THE TURNING ASIDE

The Turning Aside

*The Kingdom Poets Book
of Contemporary Christian Poetry*

Edited by

D. S. MARTIN

CASCADE *Books* · Eugene, Oregon

THE TURNING ASIDE
The Kingdom Poets Book of Contemporary Christian Poetry

Cascade Books
An Imprint of Wipf and Stock Publishers
199 W. 8th Ave., Suite 3
Eugene, OR 97401

www.wipfandstock.com

PAPERBACK ISBN: 978-1-5326-1144-5
HARDCOVER ISBN: 978-1-5326-1146-9
EBOOK ISBN: 978-1-5326-1145-2

Cataloguing-in-Publication data:

Names: Last, First. | other names in same manner

Title: Book title : book subtitle / Author Name.

Description: Eugene, OR: Cascade Books, 2016 | Series: The Poiema Poetry Series | Includes bibliographical references and index.

Identifiers: ISBN 978-1-5326-1144-5 (paperback) | ISBN 978-1-5326-1146-9 (hardcover) | ISBN 978-1-5326-1145-2 (ebook)

Subjects: LCSH: subject | subject | subject | subject

Classification: CALL NUMBER 2016 (paperback) | CALL NUMBER (ebook)

Manufactured in the U.S.A.   07/26/17

Dedicated to the encouragement of all Christian poets,
that their influence may be significant & their legacy long lasting

The tongue has the power of life and death,
and those who love it will eat its fruit.

PROVERBS 18:21

So when the Lord saw that he turned aside to look,
God called to him from the midst of the bush. . .

EXODUS 3:4

Contents

The Bright Field

I have seen the sun break through
to illuminate a small field
for a while, and gone my way
and forgotten it. But that was the pearl
of great price, the one field that had
treasure in it. I realize now
that I must give all that I have
to possess it. Life is not hurrying

on to a receding future, nor hankering after
an imagined past. It is the turning
aside like Moses to the miracle
of the lit bush, to a brightness
that seemed as transitory as your youth
once, but is the eternity that awaits you.

R.S. THOMAS

Preface
It's Time

It's time for a new anthology of contemporary Christian poetry. There have been excellent anthologies in the past, but we can no longer consider such brilliant poets as Gerard Manley Hopkins, T.S. Eliot, and C.S. Lewis as our contemporaries. Many of today's finest Christian poets were virtually unknown before we entered the new millennium. I have sought to be an encourager of poets of faith, through writing reviews for journals, through my blogs *Kingdom Poets* and *The 55 Project*, and through editing the poetry collections in the Poiema Poetry Series. This anthology arises from my love for poetic excellence by poets of faith, and my decades-long pursuit of the poetry that most speaks to my soul.

The title, *The Turning Aside*, intentionally directs the attention of readers to the R.S. Thomas poem, "The Bright Field"—to that fascinating phrase, where verb becomes noun, where Moses's experience intersects with Christ's parable, and where we are invited to participate.

Every anthology needs parameters. For this anthology of "Christian po-etry," I am focusing predominantly on poetry written by Christians. Poets included may be Evangelical, Orthodox, Protestant, Catholic, or of no particular denominational affiliation. I have not, however, asked poets to sign a statement of faith. The poems here—like those on my blog *Kingdom Poets*—are selected primarily as poems which demonstrate that the poet takes Christian faith seriously. Because we are fallible humans, we may grasp and eloquently write about truths, but potentially at the same time, or subsequently, sadly lose touch with the Master himself.

All Christians—including Christian poets—agree that Jesus Christ came as God in the flesh, he died to save sinners and rose again. If they don't believe this, they aren't Christians. Some of the poets included in this anthology wrestle with doubt more than others; some may want to distance themselves from certain groups who call themselves believers. A few might not even have clearly thought through their own theology, but have written poems that speak profoundly about our need for God. I have sought to avoid—what Donald Davie describes in his introduction to *The New Oxford Book of Christian Verse* as—poems merely with "the expression of indefinitely oceanic feelings for a something 'beyond', yeasty yearnings towards 'the transcendent'."

There are also Christian poets whose poetry rarely touches on faith; such poetry, as fine as it might be, is not the focus here. Even so, I believe that Christians are particularly enabled to speak about various aspects of what it means to be human.

In order to include the very best poetry, I chose to include a wide range of poetic styles—whether opaque or accessible, formalist or modernist, academic or populist—and to include poetry from around the world. To limit myself, I have chosen only poetry written in English by poets who were alive in January 2000. This forced me to eliminated some exceptional poets, such as Denise Levertov and Jane Kenyon who died in the 1990s, and Czeslaw Milosz who helped translate his own poetry into English. I have also sought to find a balance between established poets and worthy poets who are less known.

Christian Poetry is valuable, although *not* because it is new revelation or prophetic utterance from God (regardless of what William Blake may have believed). Just like the preachers we hear on Sunday mornings, the poets express their own ideas, as they think about scripture and the world God has made. Some of the poets may disagree with what another poet has expressed—or may disagree about ethics. I may even find that as I re-read a poem, I realize the poet is suggesting something I disagree with. Such poetry enables us to reflect on and think through what we believe. In the end we must all discern the spirits for ourselves—based on what God says, rather than on popular opinion (or the opinion of an editor). As readers, then, we may use the poems to reflect upon important truths, wrestle with difficult truths, and struggle with ideas we feel may be false.

All of these poets (with the exception of myself) have been featured on my blog Kingdom Poets. To learn more about them, to read more of their poems, and to discover other Christian poets, I provide the following web address:
www.kingdompoets.blogspot.com
A number of these poets, I am pleased to say, have had books published as part of the Poiema Poetry Series (of which I am the series editor).

Finally I encourage you to buy books by the poets whose work you most appreciate, and to share their poetry with others.

D.S. Martin—Soli Deo Gloria

Anne Porter (1911—2011) was born in Massachusetts. She neglected her poetry for years, as the wife of the painter Fairfield Porter and as mother to their children. It wasn't until well-after her husband's death in 1975 that she began to take her poetry seriously. Her first collection appeared in 1994, and her book *Living Things: Collected Poems* (Zoland Books) in 2006.

A Plea For Mercy

When I am brought before the Lord
What can I say to him
How plead for mercy?

I'll say I loved
My husband and the five
Children we had together
Though I was most unworthy

I'll say I loved
The summer mornings
I loved the way the sun comes up
And sets the dew on fire
I loved the way
The cobwebs shine
On the tall grass
When they are strung with dew

I'll say I loved
The way that little bird
The titmouse flies
I'll say I loved
Its lightness
Lilt
And beauty.

Music

When I was a child
I once sat sobbing on the floor
Beside my mother's piano
As she played and sang
For there was in her singing
A shy yet solemn glory
My smallness could not hold

And when I was asked
Why I was crying
I had no words for it
I only shook my head
And went on crying

Why is it that music
At its most beautiful
Opens a wound in us
An ache a desolation
Deep as a homesickness
For some far-off
And half-forgotten country

I've never understood
Why this is so

But there's an ancient legend
From the other side of the world
That gives away the secret
Of this mysterious sorrow

For centuries on centuries
We have been wandering
But we were made for Paradise
As deer for the forest

And when music comes to us
With its heavenly beauty
It brings us desolation
For when we hear it
We half remember
That lost native country

We dimly remember the fields
Their fragrant windswept clover
The birdsongs in the orchards
The wild white violets in the moss
By the transparent streams

And shining at the heart of it
Is the longed-for beauty
Of the One who waits for us
Who will always wait for us
In those radiant meadows

Yet also came to live with us
And wanders where we wander.

After Psalm 137

We're still in Babylon but
We do not weep
Why should we weep?
We have forgotten
How to weep

We've sold our harps
And bought ourselves machines
That do our singing for us
And who remembers now
The songs we sang in Zion?

We have got used to exile
We hardly notice
Our captivity
For some of us
There are such comforts here
Such luxuries

Even a guard
To keep the beggars
From annoying us

Jerusalem
We have forgotten you.

Another Sarah

for Christopher Smart

When winter was half over
God sent three angels to the
apple-tree
Who said to her
"Be glad, you little rack
Of empty sticks,
Because you have been chosen.

In May you will become
A wave of living sweetness
A nation of white petals
A dynasty of apples."

R.S. Thomas (1913—2000) was born in Cardiff, Wales. He spent most of his career as an Anglican priest serving rural parishioners in the Welsh hill country. His poems are often set in this landscape, among farm people. By his life's end, he was considered by many to be the most significant contemporary Welsh poet.

The Country Clergy

I see them working in old rectories
By the sun's light, by candlelight,
Venerable men, their black cloth
A little dusty, a little green
With holy mildew. And yet their skulls,
Ripening over so many prayers,
Toppled into the same grave
With oafs and yokels. They left no books,
Memorial to their lonely thought
In grey parishes; rather they wrote
On men's hearts and in the minds
Of young children sublime words
Too soon forgotten. God in his time
Or out of time will correct this.

The Empty Church

They laid this stone trap
for him, enticing him with candles,
as though he would come like some huge moth
out of the darkness to beat there.
Ah, he had burned himself
before in the human flame
and escaped, leaving the reason
torn. He will not come any more

to our lure. Why, then, do I kneel still
striking my prayers on a stone
heart? Is it in hope one
of them will ignite yet and throw
on its illumined walls the shadow
of someone greater than I can understand?

Praise

I praise you because
you are artist and scientist
in one. When I am somewhat
fearful of your power,
your ability to work miracles
with a set-square. I hear
you murmuring to yourself
in a notation Beethoven
dreamed of but never achieved.
You run off your scales of
rain water and sea water, play
the chords of the morning
and evening light, sculpture
with shadow, join together leaf
by leaf, when spring
comes, the stanzas of
an immense poem. You speak
all languages and none,
answering our most complex
prayers with the simplicity
of a flower, confronting
us, when we would domesticate you
to our uses, with the rioting
viruses under our lens.

The Hand

It was a hand. God looked at it
and looked away. There was a coldness
about his heart, as though the hand
clasped it. As at the end
of a dark tunnel, he saw cities
the hand would build, engines
that it would raze them with. His sight
dimmed. Tempted to undo the joints
of the fingers, he picked it up.
But the hand wrestled with him. "Tell
me your name," it cried, "and I will write it
in bright gold. Are there not deeds
to be done, children to make, poems
to be written. The world
is without meaning, awaiting
my coming." But God, feeling the nails
in his side, the unnerving warmth
of the contact, fought on in
silence. This was the long war with himself
always foreseen, the question not
to be answered. What is the hand
for? The immaculate conception
preceding the delivery
of the first tool? "I let you go,"
he said, "but without blessing.
Messenger to the mixed things
Of your making, tell them I am."

The Absence

It is this great absence
that is like a presence, that compels
me to address it without hope
of a reply. It is a room I enter
from which someone has just
gone, the vestibule for the arrival
of one who has not yet come.
I modernise the anachronism
of my language, but he is no more here
than before. Genes and molecules
have no more power to call
him up than the incense of the Hebrews
at their altars. My equations fail
as my words do. What resources have I
other than the emptiness without him of my whole
being, a vacuum he may not abhor?

The Other

There are nights that are so still
that I can hear the small owl calling
far off and a fox barking
miles away. It is then that I lie
in the lean hours awake listening
to the swell born somewhere in the Atlantic
rising and falling, rising and falling
wave on wave on the long shore
by the village that is without light
and companionless. And the thought comes
of that other being who is awake, too,
letting our prayers break on him,
not like this for a few hours,
but for days, years, for eternity.

C.H. Sisson (1914—2003) was born in Bristol, where he was raised in the Methodist Church. He transferred his allegiance to the Church of England and became dedicated to traditional Anglicanism. Carcanet published his *Collected Poems* in 1984, and in 1998. In 1993 he received a Companion of Honour for his poetry.

The Usk

> *Christ is the language in which we speak to God*
> *And also God, therefore we speak in truth;*
> *He in us, we in Him, speaking*
> *To one another, to Him, the City of God.*

I.
Such a fool as I am you had better ignore
Tongue twist, malevolent, fat mouthed
I have no language but that other one
His the Devil's, no mouse I, creeping out of the cheese
With a peaked cap scanning the distance
Looking for truth.
Words when I have them, come out, the Devil
Encouraging, grinning from the other side of the street
And my tears
Streaming, a blubbered face, when I am not laughing
Where in all this
Is calm, measure,
Exactness
The Lord's peace?

II.
Nothing is in my own voice because I have not
Any. Nothing in my own name
Here inscribed on water, nothing but flow
A ripple, outwards. Standing beside the Usk
You flow like truth, river, I will get in

Over me, through me perhaps, river let me be crystalline
As I shall not be, shivering upon the bank.
A swan passed. So is it, the surface, sometimes
Benign like a mirror, but not I passing, the bird.

III.
Under the bridge, meet reward, the water
Falling in cascades or worse, you devil, for truthfulness
Is no part of the illusion, the clear sky
Is not yours, the water
Falling not yours
Only the sheep
Munching at the river brim
Perhaps

IV.
What I had hoped for, the clear line
Tremulous like water but
Clear also to the stones underneath
Has not come that way, for my truth
Was not public enough, nor perhaps true.
Holy Father, Almighty God
Stop me before I speak

                            — per Christum.

V.
Lies on my tongue. Get up and bolt the door
For I am coming not to be believed
The messenger of anything I say.
So I am come, stand in the cold tonight
The servant of the grain upon my tongue,
Beware, I am the man, and let me in.

VI.
So speech is treasured, for the things it gives
Which I can not have, for I speak too plain
Yet not so plain as to be understood.
It is confusion and a madman's tongue.

Where drops the reason, there is no one by.
Torture my mind: and so swim through the night
As envy cannot touch you, or myself
Sleep comes, and let her, warm at my side, like death.
The Holy Spirit and the Holy One
Of Israel be my guide. So among tombs
Truth may be sought, and found, if we rejoice
With Ham and Shem and Japhet in the dark.
The ark rolls onward over a wide sea.
Come sleep, come lightening, comes the dove at last.

Easter

One good crucifixion and he rose from the dead
He knew better than to wait for age
To nibble his intellect
And depress his love.

Out in the desert the sun beats and the cactus
Prickles more fiercely than any in his wilderness
And his forty days
Were merely monastic.

What he did on the cross was no more
Than others have done for less reason
And the resurrection you could take for granted.

What is astonishing is that he came here at all
Where no one ever came voluntarily before.

On the Prayer Book

The empty bucket, sound, clangs in the well
And draws up nothing, banged against the wall.
Was meaning down there? It is dry now
And all around the well-head chirrup and mow
Empty figures of silken Why and How.

David Gascoyne (1916—2001) was born in London. In the 1930s in Paris, he befriended Salvador Dali, and became associated with the surrealist movement. His later poetry, however, became metaphysical, and focused on his faith. His *New Selected Poems* (Enitharmon Press) appeared in 1995.

Ecce Homo

Whose is this horrifying face,
This putrid flesh, discoloured, flayed,
Fed on by flies, scorched by the sun?
Whose are these hollow red-filmed eyes
And thorn-spiked head and spear-stuck side?
Behold the Man: He is Man's Son.

Forget the legend, tear the decent veil
That cowardice or interest devised
To make their mortal enemy a friend,
To hide the bitter truth all His wounds tell,
Lest the great scandal be no more disguised:
He is in agony till the world's end,

And we must never sleep during that time!
He is suspended on the cross-tree now
And we are onlookers at the crime,
Callous contemporaries of the slow
Torture of God. Here is the hill
Made ghastly by His spattered blood

Whereon He hangs and suffers still:
See, the centurions wear riding-boots,
Black shirts and badges and peaked caps,
Greet one another with raised-arm salutes;
They have cold eyes, unsmiling lips;
Yet these His brothers know not what they do.

And on his either side hang dead

A labourer and a factory hand,
Or one is maybe a lynched Jew
And one a Negro or a Red,
Coolie or Ethiopian, Irishman,
Spaniard or German democrat.

Behind his lolling head the sky
Glares like a fiery cataract
Red with the murders of two thousand years
Committed in His name and by
Crusaders, Christian warriors
Defending faith and property.

Amid the plain beneath His transfixed hands,
Exuding darkness as indelible
As guilty stains, fanned by funereal
And lurid airs, besieged by drifting sands
And clefted landslides our about-to-be
Bombed and abandoned cities stand.

He who wept for Jerusalem
Now sees His prophecy extend
Across the greatest cities of the world,
A guilty panic reason cannot stem
Rising to raze them all as He foretold;
And He must watch this drama to the end.

Though often named, He is unknown
To the dark kingdoms at His feet
Where everything disparages His words,
And each man bears the common guilt alone
And goes blindfolded to his fate,
And fear and greed are sovereign lords.

The turning point of history
Must come. Yet the complacent and the proud
And who exploit and kill, may be denied—
Christ of Revolution and of Poetry—

The resurrection and the life
Wrought by your spirit's blood.

Involved in their own sophistry
The black priest and the upright man
Faced by subversive truth shall be struck dumb,
Christ of Revolution and of Poetry,
While the rejected and condemned become
Agents of the divine.

Not from a monstrance silver-wrought
But from the tree of human pain
Redeem our sterile misery,
Christ of Revolution and of Poetry,
That man's long journey
May not have been in vain.

Pieta

Stark in the pasture on the skull-shaped hill,
In swollen aura of disaster shrunken and
Unsheltered by the ruin of the sky,
Intensely concentrated in themselves the banded
Saints abandoned kneel.

And under the unburdened tree
Great in their midst, the rigid folds
Of a blue cloak upholding as a text
Her grief-scrawled face for the ensuing world to read,
The Mother, whose dead Son's dear head
Weighs like a precious blood-incrusted stone
On her unfathomable breast:

Holds Him God has forsaken, Word made flesh
Made ransom, to the slow smoulder of her heart
Till the catharsis of the race shall be complete.

Margaret Avison (1918—2007) lived most of her life in Toronto. She twice received the Governor General's Award for poetry, and is an Officer of the Order of Canada. Her book *Concrete and Wild Carrot* (2002) received the Griffin Poetry Prize. Avison is known for her sometimes-difficult, philosophical poetry—respected both for, and in spite of, its focus on Christian faith.

Leading Questions

Walking naked in Eden, they
lived always in the light
of the holy. Drawn to disobey
they awoke to shame—and God-

like comprehension of pain,
of broken as well as good,
(What would our choice have been
if we had understood?)

And what was the shame about?
And why did He need, then,
to 'clothe the lilies', who night–
ly met those unclad in Eden?

Had nakedness not meant freedom?
At evening, now forsaken
by our choice, was that to Him
as since to us, heartbreaking?

Yet He taught the Jews to weave
rich fabrics for the abode
He would live in, or above
in fire or (covering) cloud,

and long since He has promised to prepare
for us the robe He hopes His guests that Day will wear.

On a Maundy Thursday Walk

The Creator was
walking by the sea, the
Holy Book says. Finely-tuned
senses — flooded with
intense awareness — tested
a clear serene constancy.

Who can imagine it, sullied
as our senses are? Faulty as are even out
most excellent makings?

The perfection of
created Being, in the perfect
morning was born from the walker-by-the-sea's
imagination. At a word —
the hot smell of sunned rock, of
the sea, the sea, the sound of lapping, bird-calls,
the sifting sponginess of sand
under the sandals, delicate.
April light—all, at a word
had become this almost-
overwhelming loveliness.

Surely the exultation —
the Artist
Himself immersed in
His work, finding it flawless —
intensified the so soon
leaving (lifted out of
mortal life for good
forever).

That too eludes
us who disbelieve that we
also shall say goodbye to

trees and cherished friends and
sunsets and crunching snow
to travel off
into a solo death.

How much more, that
(suffering this
creation to go under
its Maker, and us all)
He, the Father of love, should stake it all
on a sufficient
indeed on an essential
pivot.

What John Saw (Revelation 4)

The black holes out there, of pure (physical) force
in the heavens,
those in-and-out plosions, focused,
remote, in the rhythm of
incomprehensible infrequency
but nonetheless in time,
speak the extremes absolute of a rhythm
we mortals know.
They are like us contained in
creation's 'Let it be so.'

Who can comprehend, with a heart hungry
for meaning?
who does not feel the uprooting
tremor of one event —
one person's, or , in the stupefying
astronomers' book of hours, one
pulse of the megalorhythm?

Yes   yes   I know
this bronzing beech tree, the
blackening myrtle at its foot
(event in all my seasons,
seasoned for this long before I was
born) exists in a mere
twitch, is rushing towards the node
millennia away, just one episode.
Time curls on itself.

Least moments given, though,
can open onto
John's comprehender: here,
there, then, always
now, because unchanging, who made light and ponderous rhythms,
time and all
pulsing particulars.
John saw him rainbowed in glory —
compact of all our music, hearing the farthest
compositions, and the most intricately
present. Magnet. Intensifier. Agonizingly
rediscoverering, in shards, the shapes
design is satisfied to see.
One. White. Whole.

Secrets within
all that John saw
in the bronzing beech tree
of this October twilight
though I do not yet see,
even in mind, being
not yet out of time.

Cliff Ashby (1919—2012) was born in Norfolk, England. His first collection *In the Vulgar Tongue*, did not appear until 1968. Despite not being well known, Cliff Ashby has been called one of the foremost poets of his generation. He is one of the few contemporary poets Donald Davie featured in *The New Oxford Book of Christian Verse* (1981).

Latter Day Psalms

1

Somewhere there is Grace, Lord,
Was I not told it as a child
When the sound of the sparrow
Filled my heart with delight
And the rain fell like friendship on my head.
Now the call of the cuckoo
Cannot calm my aching heart
And my soul is tormented with fear.
Have mercy, Lord, for I have travelled far
Yet all my knowledge is as nothing.
My days are numbered. Time titters
As I stumble down the street.
Forgiveness, O forgive me, Lord,
Close my critical eye
Take me to your breast
For how else may I die.

2

The tree waves in the wind
But does not break unless
The bough is over-burdened.
When spring disrupts the dead days
Buds, leaves, and birds praise God
In song and silent sound.
The dead dock, stiff
With last year's pride,
Leans unwillingly in the gale.

My heart, Lord, is unyielding.
My joints are stiff
The knuckles of my knees
Refuse to bend.
The knife is at my neck,
My back breaks.
I will say my matutinal prayers
From a crippled position,
Perhaps the Lord will hear?

3
I lived among lewd men
Beneath the Crouch End clock
Waiting for God to speak.
But my ears were dull
And what my brain received
My mind misunderstood.
So I took my mean heart to the hills,
Beside the Palace of Alexandra
Gazed on Barbican and grieved.
Lord speak to me in the morning
Or the night will be everlasting.
Now all the dogs of Dewsbury
Bay about my heels
And the foul water of the Calder
Weeps into the sea.

4
On the estate, Lord, the people
Take counsel one with another
And in the public house
There is lamentation.
The cost of living soars
Like wild duck rising
After morning feed.
Man has neither means nor meaning.
The cry of the young in the street
Rouses a protest in the market place.

What shall I do, Lord?
Though I bring my sad soul
And place it at Your feet,
My mouth is bitter, for fear
Infects my hand and heart.
The pit of hell yawns wide
Before my floundering feet,
I slip, I slide, I fall,
I try to grasp a skylark
But it flies south for summer.
My mind is melancholic,
I cannot praise my maker.

Madeline DeFrees was born in Oregon in 1919. She spent 38 years as a Catholic nun before retiring to concentrate on her writing. She has twice received Washington State Book Awards: for her poetry collections *Blue Dusk* (2001) and *Spectral Waves*, (2006)—both from Copper Canyon Press.

Psalm for a New Nun

My life was rescued like a bird from the fowler's snare.
It comes back singing tonight in my loosened hair

as I bend to the mirror in this contracted room
lit by the electric music of the comb.

With hair cropped close as a boy's, contained in a coif,
I let years make me forget what I had cut off.

Now the glass cannot compass my dark halo
and the frame censors the dense life it cannot follow.

Like strength restored in the temple this sweetness wells
quietly into tissues of abandoned cells;

better by as much as it is better
to be a woman, I feel this gradual urgency

till the comb snaps, the mirror widens, and the walls recede.
With head uncovered I am no longer afraid.

Broken is the snare and I am freed.
My help is in the Lord who made
heaven and earth. Yes, earth.

The Eye

Lodged in a bony orbit in the skull, the eye
is slower than the hand
and more inclined to doubt in spite of
what the ole saw claims: *Seeing is believing.*
this was not the case with skeptic
Thomas, who put his unbelieving hand
into the Master's wounded side

                                   and only then
declared his faith. I trust the eye: it winnows
wheat from chaff. And in the furnace, separates
true metal from slag. An eye for minimal
upheaval proves a mode of second
sight: the anthill army's small
earth-moving crew. Wrought-iron handrails

filigreed with spider-cloth, sequined with dew.
Half-open clematis against
a chain-link fence, their creamy lemon
shading into white. Blue-black sky
swept clean with brushwork in the evening
light and winter-bare japonica's faint
flush of green before the leaves come out.

Because the eyes are windows on the soul, wise
men close the curtain. Hoard rivers of bright
color. When words arrive with hearts
pinned to their sleeve, the brave will plunge
the writing hand into the right-brain
wound to draw out blood and water
the doubter can believe.

Skid Row

Out of the depths have I cried, O Lord,
Where the lean heart preys on the hardened crust.
Where short wicks falter on candle-hopes
And winter whips at a patchwork trust.

From darkened doorways no welcome shines,
No promise waits up the broken stair,
And the coin that summons the night with wine
Buys a morning of sick despair.

Out of the depths have I cried in vain
And the still streets echo my lonely calls;
All the long night in the moaning wind
The bruised reed breaks and the sparrow falls.

Richard Wilbur was born in New York City in 1921. His poetry primarily follows traditional poetic structures, despite the prominence of the modernists. He has received many honors—including twice winning the Pulitzer Prize, and in 1987 being appointed Poet Laureate of the United States. His recent poetry collection *Anterooms* (2010) was published by Houghton Mifflin Harcourt.

Love Calls Us To The Things Of This World

The eyes open to a cry of pulleys,
And spirited from sleep, the astounded soul
Hangs for a moment bodiless and simple
As false dawn.
                Outside the open window
The morning air is all awash with angels.

Some are in bed-sheets, some are in blouses,
Some are in smocks: but truly there they are.
Now they are rising together in calm swells
Of halcyon feeling, filling whatever they wear
With the deep joy of their impersonal breathing;

Now they are flying in place, conveying
The terrible speed of their omnipresence, moving
And staying like white water; and now of a sudden
They swoon down in so rapt a quiet
That nobody seems to be there.
                   The soul shrinks

From all that it is about to remember,
From the punctual rape of every blessed day,
And cries,
            "Oh, let there be nothing on
   earth but laundry,
Nothing but rosy hands in the rising steam
And clear dances done in the sight of heaven."

26

Yet, as the sun acknowledges
With a warm look the world's hunks and colors,
The soul descends once more in bitter love
To accept the waking body, saying now
In a changed voice as the man yawns and rises,

"Bring them down from their ruddy gallows;
Let there be clean linen for the backs of thieves;
Let lovers go fresh and sweet to be undone,
And the heaviest nuns walk in a pure floating
Of dark habits,
                 keeping their difficult balance."

A Wedding Toast

St. John tells how, at Cana's wedding feast,
The water-pots poured wine in such amount
That by his sober count
There were a hundred gallons at the least.

It made no earthly sense, unless to show
How whatsoever love elects to bless
Brims to a sweet excess
That can without depletion overflow.

Which is to say that what love sees is true;
That this world's fullness is not made but found.
Life hungers to abound
And pour its plenty out for such as you.

Now, if your loves will lend an ear to mine,
I toast you both, good son and dear new daughter.
May you not lack for water,
And may that water smack of Cana's wine.

27

Matthew Viii, 28 ff

Rabbi, we Gadarenes
Are not ascetics; we are fond of wealth and possessions.
Love, as You call it, we obviate by means
Of the planned release of aggressions.

We have deep faith in prosperity.
Soon, it is hoped, we will reach our full potential.
In the light of our gross product, the practice of charity
Is palpably non-essential.

It is true that we go insane;
That for no good reason we are possessed by devils;
That we suffer, despite the amenities which obtain
At all but the lowest levels.

We shall not, however, resign
Our trust in the high-heaped table and the full trough.
If You cannot cure us without destroying our swine,
We had rather You shoved off.

A Christmas Hymn

A stable-lamp is lighted
Whose glow shall wake the sky;
The stars shall bend their voices,
And every stone shall cry.
And every stone shall cry,
And straw like gold shall shine;
A barn shall harbor heaven,
A stall become a shrine.

This child through David's city
Shall ride in triumph by;
The palm shall strew its branches,
And every stone shall cry.
And every stone shall cry,
Though heavy, dull, and dumb,
And lie within the roadway
To pave His kingdom come.

Yet He shall be forsaken,
And yielded up to die;
The sky shall groan and darken,
And every stone shall cry.
And every stone shall cry
For stony hearts of men:
God's blood upon the spearhead,
God's love refused again.

But now, as at the ending,
The low is lifted high;
The stars shall bend their voices,
And every stone shall cry.
And every stone shall cry
In praises of the child
By whose descent among us
The worlds are reconciled.

Elizabeth Jennings (1926—2001) lived most of her life in Oxford. She is the author of more than two dozen volumes of poetry, mostly published by Macmillan and Carcanet. They demonstrate her lyrical style and mastery of poetic forms. In 1992 she became a Commander of the Order of the British Empire (CBE).

The Nature of Prayer

(a debt to Van Gogh's "Crooked Church")

Maybe a mad fit made you set it there
Askew, bent to the wind, the blue-print gone
Awry, or did it? Isn't every prayer
We say oblique, unsure, seldom a simple one,
Shaken as your stone tightening in the air?

Decorum smiles a little. Columns, domes
Are sights, are aspirations. We can't dwell
For long among such loftiness. Our homes
Of prayer are shaky and, yes, parts of Hell
Fragment the depths from which the great cry comes.

Friday

We nailed the hands long ago,
Wove the thorns, took up the scourge and shouted
For excitement's sake, we stood at the dusty edge
Of the pebbled path and watched the extreme of pain.

But one or two prayed, one or two
Were silent, shocked, stood back
And remembered remnants of words, a new vision,
The cross is up with its crying victim, the clouds

Cover the sun, we learn a new way to lose
What we did not know we had
Until this bleak and sacrificial day,
Until we turned from our bad
Past and knelt and cried out our dismay,
The dice still clicking, the voices dying away.

The Resurrection

I was the one who waited in the garden
Doubting the morning and the early light.
I watched the mist lift off its own soft burden,
Permitting not believing my own sight.

If there were sudden noises I dismissed
Them as a trick of sound, a sleight of hand.
Not by a natural joy could I be blessed
Or trust a thing I could not understand.

Maybe I was a shadow thrown by some
Who, weeping , came to lift away the stone,
Or was I but the path on which the sun
Too heavy for itself, was loosed and thrown?

I heard the voices and the recognition
And love like kisses heard behind the walls.
Were they my tears which fell, a real contrition?
Or simply April with its waterfalls?

It was by negatives I learned my place.
The garden went on growing and I sensed
A sudden breeze that blew across my face.
Despair returned but now it danced, it danced.

Rod Jellema was born in Michigan in 1927. He is Professor Emeritus of English at the University of Maryland, where he founded the Creative Writing Program. His Collected Poems, *Incarnality*—his fifth poetry book—appeared from Eerdmans in 2010. He has also translated two volumes of Frisian poetry. He lives in Washington, D.C.

Letter to Lewis Smedes About God's Presence

Dear Lew,

I have to look in cracks and crevices.
Don't tell me how God's mercy
is as wide as the ocean, as deep as the sea.
I already believe it, but that infinite prospect
gets farther away the more we mouth it.
I thank you for lamenting his absences —
from marriages going mad, from the deaths
of your son and mine, from the inescapable
terrors of history: Treblinka. Viet Nam.
September Eleven. It's hard to celebrate
his invisible Presence in the sacrament
while seeing his visible absence from the world.

This must be why mystics and poets record
the slender incursions of splintered light,
echoes, fragments, odd words and phrases
like flashes through darkened hallways.
These stabs remind me that the proud
and portly old church is really only
that cut green slip grafted into a tiny nick
that merciful God himself slit into the stem
of his chosen Judah. The thin and tenuous
thread we hang by, so astonishing,
is the metaphor I need at the shoreline
of all those immeasurable oceans of love.

Adapted from an e-mail discussion, Summer 2002

We Used to Grade God's Sunsets from the Lost Valley Beach

Why we really watched we never said.
The play of spectral light, but maybe also
the coming dark, and the need to trust
that the fire dying down before us
into Lake Michigan's cold waves
would rise again behind us.
Our arch and witty critiques
covered our failures to say what we saw.

The madcap mockery of grading God as though
He were a struggling student artist
(Cut loose, strip it down, study Matisse
and risk something, something unseen —
C-plus, keep trying — that sort of thing)
only hid our fear of His weather
howling through the galaxies. We humored
a terrible truth: that nature gives us hope
only in flashes, split seconds, one
at a time, fired in a blaze of beauty.

Picking apart those merely actual sunsets,
we stumbled into knowing the artist's job:
to sort out, then to seize and work an insight
until it's transformed into permanence.
And God, brushing in for us the business
of clouds and sky, really is a hawker
of clichés, a sentimental hack as a painter.
He means to be. He leaves it to us
to catch and revise, to find the forms
of how and who in this world we really are
and would be, to see how much promise there is
on a hurtling planet, swung from a thread
of light and saved by nothing but grace.

Take A Chance

If you cancel the trip to Innesfree
because it's raining, you may miss the quick
red rage of a torn leaf
before it gentles itself onto the quiet pool.

The tests warned him that his exceptional mind
was weakest for doing math, so math
is what he took up with holy awe,
forcing his dazzled way to insight.

If you always leave a nightlight burning
because as a child you got fearfully lost,
turn it off. The lights far out in the dark
are sending lifelines you never imagined.

The New Age seers, tracking the fates, may tell you
no — but take a chance. Just maybe that old
unbelievable Yahweh really did imprint you
with enough God Image to make you free to leap.

Take This Cup

The flash of red he poured in their cups, squeezed
from flesh of bursting grapes in proud Judean vineyards,
was wine passed among them for centuries
in joyful celebrations, with dancing and music —
and he called it "my blood."
And he said, "Remember me."

Remember me, he surely meant, *always,*
but also a few hours from then, when they,
drowsy mortals falling asleep in earth's night,
could not help him pray his way free
from the thought of a more terrible cup,
a cup thick and bitter enough to gag him.

Today, Friday, as he hangs by his wounds from a cross,
he might settle for that second cup, a cup of anything,
a thimbleful, a stick to suck. Struggling to cry out
from a swollen throat scorched by God›s anger —
anger not with him who hangs there but with us —
he rasps two thick-tongued words: *I thirst.*

Two words from Immanuel, from «God-with-us,»
two words choked out through human flesh.
Behold the bodily drag and heft of redemption,
earned not by heavenward flights we rise to
but by his having descended. What matters is not
the spirituality of humans. It's the humanity of God.

Well, it›s Friday. Two more days before we
 stare into abstract space, trying to think, or otherwise
shout and raise our cups, click our glasses brimming
with wine that breathes out soul and spirit
 while giving our needy mouths the smack of earthy,
 full-bodied love for which we were created.

Holy Saturday

Nothing possible can save us.

(W. H. Auden)

Here it is again, Saturday,
Holy Week at an end.
Friday's event has shut down
the mind, left it

 beaten, slain and entombed
in dark, suspended
 between death and a wholly
impossible Sunday.

Yet the mind insists it could
move, roll the stone away
from the mouth, squint again
into what blazes out there, then

shout aloud or hum the melodies
of morning birds, choirs, bells
that easter their way into total amazement.

Come Sunday. Hurry.

Luci Shaw was born in London in 1928, but has also lived in Canada, Australia and the US. Her numerous books include the poetry collection *Scape* (Poiema Poetry Series, 2013) and *Sea Glass: New and Selected* Poems (WordFarm, 2016). Since 1988 she has been Writer in Residence at Regent College in Vancouver. She is the recipient of the 2013 Denise Levertov Award, and lives in Bellingham, Washington.

Flathead Lake, Montana

> *"Christ plays in ten thousand places"*
>
> Gerard. Manley Hopkins

Lying here on the short grass, I am
a bowl for sunlight.

Silence. A bee. The lip lip of water
over stones. The swish and slap, hollow

under the dock. Down-shore
a man sawing wood.

Christ in the sunshine laughing
through the green translucent wings

of maple seeds. A bird
resting its song on two notes.

Spring, St, Martin's Chapel, Cathedral of St. John the Divine

> for *Madeleine L'Engle*

Both of us kneel, then wait

on the church chairs—square, chocolate brown—
knowing that soon the black priest

will hurry in, wearing his lateness like
the wrong robe. In the pregnant emptiness
before communion, that crack between worlds,

we listen inward, feet tight on the cold slate,
wanting to hear Christ tell us Feed on me.
Our hearts shiver, hidden. Nothing visible moves.

Outside a drizzle starts; drops spit on the sill.
The window bird flies motionless in
a cobalt sky of skillful glass.

But beyond the frame, plucking the eye
like a message from Outside, a minor shadow
tilts and swoops in light rain,

wings telling us to fly wide, loose
and nervy as sparrows who may peck crumbs from
any picnic table, or gnats right out of the air.

Present

At light-speed, God-speed,
time collapses into *now* so that
we may see Christ's wounds as
still bleeding, his torso,
that ready sponge, still
absorbing our vice, our toxic shame.

He is still being pierced
by every hateful nail
we hammer home. In this
Golgotha moment his body—

chalice for the dark weeping
of the whole world—brims,

spilling over as his lifeblood
drains. His dying into the earth
begins the great reversal—
as blood from a vein leaps
into the needle, so with his rising,
we surge into light.

So It Is With the Spirit

How secretly the bones move
    under the skin
and the veins thread their way
    through their forests, the trees
of bones, the mosses of cells,
    the muscle vines.
How privately the ears
    tune themselves to music heard
only in the echoing cave of the head.
    And the tongue in its grotto tests
the bitterness of unripe fruit, and wine,
    the mouth feel of honey in the comb.
How cunningly our shadows
    follow us as we walk.
And our breath, how it moves in
    and out without great thought.
Even rain, which needs no summons from us
    but flows, a gift from heaven,
as the grasses rise greenly, shivering.
    Just so, beauty besieges us
unannounced, invading us, saving our souls.
    So it is with the Spirit.

Mary Considers Her Situation

What next, she wonders,
with the angel disappearing, and her room
suddenly gone dark.

The loneliness of her news
possesses her. She ponders
how to tell her mother.

Still, the secret at her heart burns like
a sun rising. How to hold it in—
that which cannot be contained.

She nestles into herself, half-convinced
it was some kind of good dream,
she its visionary.

But then, part dazzled, part prescient—
she hugs her body, a pod with a seed
that will split her.

Verb

A poem dredges for meanings
from the mud at the bottom of a
tidal mind.

A word—an eyelash, a nipple, a toenail,
an earlobe—a scrap attached to
something larger.
Letters strung together
turn strong enough to kick open a door or
nudge it closed with one finger.

It takes only a coin or a thumbnail, to block
the sun. A fly on the glass. A tree twig.
The slat of a window blind.

In the shadow cave, the sudden
spark of a single candle
heightens the mystery.

How well the world could work without me.
What reason is there for any of us to be
thrust into being by a word?

What I Needed to Do

I made for grief a leaden bowl
    and drank it, every drop.
And though I thought I'd downed it all
    the hurting didn't stop.

I made of hope a golden sieve
    to drain my world of pain.
Though I was sure I'd bled it dry
    the void filled up again.

I made of words a silver fork
    and stabbed love in the heart,
and when I found the sweetness gone
    I chewed it into art.

Collection, Recollection

Can the arrow forget the bow-string
and the bow, their pent-up passion
to let fly? The sudden snap and twang,

the relief of release?

The fledgling, having just
chipped herself free into the nest,
how does she practice
the wide threat of space?

A clear lens, the drop of rain
carries in its orb an image of the sky
from which it fell—a piece of cloud—and
with it a recollection of thunder.

And the predestined satchel
of tomorrow, how can it not be packed
with the finely-orchestrated
chaos of today?

Thunder and Then

Thunder and then the rain comes and the
prairie that has been baked dry and the
shriveled grass and the ground that has
thirsted all summer open like mouths as
the wet arrives at first in whispers and
then in sheets of silver arrows that tear the
air and join like the clapping of hands to
a downfall that makes splashes in the dirt
and grows to pools that shine in the silver light
and the dry creeks with their stones begin to
thank God for sending water for their need
so that there is praise in the rushing streams
and the trees also raise praise with their leaves
flashing and now wind like a fist takes hold of the
house and shakes it and us and it seems that
all the world is drowning in the delight of deluge.

Sarah Klassen was born in Manitoba in 1932. She is one of Canada's most-significant Mennonite writers—having published seven poetry books, including *Monstrance* (Turnstone, 2012) and several books of fiction, including her novel, *The Wittenbergs* (Turnstone, 2013). She has received many honors, such as the Canadian Authors Association Award for poetry.

First Day of Creation

Let there be light! A flash, a bolt, a brilliant blaze
that puts the kibosh on chaos. Let light shine on width, breadth,
depth, a dazzle to illuminate all matter everywhere. Let it glint
gloriously off ocean wave, sea swell, a brooklet's little ripples.

Let fish rejoice in it fantastically, the fur of fox, cat, cougar,
coyote be haloed. Let light's hot pulse pull prairie grass, kinnikinnik
up, up to verdant growth, turn grain from green to gold.
In every garden everywhere let peonies, nasturtiums and

preposterous begonias unfold. Let every butterfly, bat, bird
bathe in radiance. Let it pour mornings into breakfast bowls,
fill empty cups to overflowing. At evening let light's long plumes
linger: violet and vivid on every atom of creation.

When darkness closes in, shrouding the valley floor,
let sky be spangled still, lit with the glow of meteors,
the murky milky way, the white hot stars. O Light of life,
Light of the wobbling world: your splendor does not tarnish,

will not be overcome by random avalanche,
smart missile, guns, flood, smoke of forest fire.
Your warmth will melt the iron grip of fear.
A stone-cold guarded grave can never hold you.

In The Garden

Then God said, "Let us make humankind
in our image. . ." (Genesis 1:26)

What were you thinking, God? In spring
the boulevards strut their tenderest green
spun in your brain. Tantalizing birdsong,
fragrances float straight to the head. The heart,
as you well know, falters.
We'll regularly fail to tend the garden,
forget to feed the animals. Apples
will be wasted. How extravagantly

beautiful the blossoms are on shrubs and trees
in May. Impatient, we want fruit, not green,
but glowing. Want to sink our teeth
into the flesh of apricots. Out tongues crave
taste of apples.

What were you thinking, leaving us in charge,
giving us dominion, as if we were fit
to be emperors, chief executives, micro or macro
managers, as if we understood
words like *tend, wait patiently* and *multiply*?

As if we were able with our wayward minds
to imagine mercy's breadth and wideness,
had ears to hear, could learn to linger
long enough to taste and see.

Credo

I wanted the soprano
when she sang Handel's aria
not to be alarmed by the intruding
street noises, heat, the unrelenting
worms that one day will destroy
her body and mine.
I wanted her to disregard latecomers
trust the technique she had so far
and so well mastered.
I wanted her to believe the incredible
phrases she sang flawlessly:
> *I know that my redeemer liveth*
> *And in my flesh*
> *Shall I see God.*

In the stifling sanctuary's
last, shadowed row
I wanted
(as the thirsty deer wants water)
to believe it too.

Horizon

It isn't easy writing a poem
about Jesus. You could write the sun
hung low over olive groves
an ancient well in a quaint village
even angels into the landscape.
And blood. But his hard words
his terrible naked mercy
hang like an awkwardness
across a gaunt horizon. His name won't fit
the line's rhythm

unless you make it an expletive
or shape it like a sweet
innocuous philosophy.

It is possible
a poem would lay bare his face
his torn hands
invoke his voice   a hammer
or a bell shattering the crystal morning
at the water's edge
speaking your name and asking
do you love me.

Ritual

Holy Week and three buffleheads on the cold river
 practise the rite of baptism. Their preference:
complete immersion. Again and again they duck
and disappear into ice-cold darkness, then emerge, shaking
a zillion stars from their feathers. As if there is never enough
purification, they plunge down deep and rise and dive
and rise again.
The week winds down, down
down toward Friday. Temple draperies are torn.
Darkness enfolds the earth. The dead in their stone tombs
are stirring as if, like the sun in the morning,
they will rise.

Eugene H. Peterson was born in Washington State in 1932. He was a pastor at Christ Our King Presbyterian Church in Maryland for 29 years, and is Professor Emeritus of Spiritual Theology at Regent College in Vancouver. He is best known for *The Message*—his popular paraphrase of the Bible. His poetry collection *Holy Luck* (Eerdmans) appeared in 2013.

Assateague Island

> *All thy waves and billows*
> *Have gone over me.*
>
> Psalm 42:7

A double-crested cormorant,
  Brobdingnagian duck, black
On green, cushioned by six or seven
  Inches of air above the killing
Billows, wings a swift passage
  Through the wet wave troughs.

Beneath the bird water gathers and crests
  In curved mandalas, crashes in mantra
Chants, then slides down the strand
  Into the deep where ocean spray
Is recollected in the great
  Salt, billow-making womb.

Effortless elegance!
  Holy wildness!

We walked nine miles of ocean beach
  Yesterday and let the ocean
Rhythms—pulse-setting waves and tide-making
  Moon—get inside us. Slowed
By this ancient pacemaker
  Our hearts thirsted. We drank God.

Edwin Thumboo was born in Singapore in 1933. He is Emeritus Professor and Professorial Fellow at the National University of Singapore, and has been a visiting Professor in the US, UK, Austria, Australia, Malaysia and Hong Kong. *The Best of Edwin Thumboo* was published by Epigram Books in 2012.

Fall & Redemption

I.
I bit sin; tasted apple. A piece stuck in my
Throat for me to feel for us to remember
This start, this shame, before the
                    Tree of Life:
Holy, blossoming, its fire-cherubim up front.
Our Garden changed, those serpent-years ago.
No more sharing gentle evenings with Him.
Yet, my God, as you judged, banished, drove us
East of Eden, you yet gave skin-garments made

Of loving kindness, for us to settle, grow, herd;
Coax planted dust t raise again; for our sheep
To graze, awaiting the whitest Lamb.
                    But O Abel!
O jealous Cain! As you slit your brother's blood,
You surely spill your own. My sin yet flows from
That first bite, killing flesh of my flesh and, surely,
My brother's keeper too. I cry to High Heaven,
Lamenting bitterly till tears run dry. No respite.

Yet God knew this blood is saved through Blood
That sat by Him from the foundation of the world.

II.
And He came Star-bright, fulfilling prophesy,
Grew in His Father's house; John B baptised;
Defeated the Devil, was Transfigured:

This is my beloved
Son in whom I am well pleased. Hear him.
And they heard, still hear, as He gathered His
Twelve, preaching love; forgiveness. Turn
Your left cheek, embrace your enemies, share
Your bounty, humble yourselves, cleave to the

                Holy Spirit; hearken unto
                The Sermon on the Mount; The Beatitudes
                From Everlasting to Everlasting.

You made water wine; asked the lame to walk—
They walked; the blind to see—they saw. Infinite
Mercy and Faithfulness, King, Redeemer,
              Sacrifice:
You gave all, all, as they hit the last nail, as the soldier
Pushed his spear into your side. Blood-bleeding
Washed away our sins. The Man in you cried *E-'li,*
E-'li la'-ma sa-bach'-tha-ni. It is finished. Father, INTO
THY HANDS I COMMEND MY SPIRIT.

We adore the Ever—
Living God, Resurrected Christ, I Am that I AM
Who rose on the Third Day, appeared to Disciples,
Then opened the Heavens,
The Way and The Life. . .

Gods Can Die

I have seen powerful men
Undo themselves, keep two realities
One for minor friends, one for the powers that be,
The really powerful. Such people take a role
Supporting managers of state,
Accept an essential part in some minor project.
But after a bit of duty,

That makes them fester with intentions,
They play the major figure to old friends.

We understand and try to seek a balance in the dark
To know the private from the public monument,
To find our way between the private and the public
argument
Or what *can* be said or if a thing is meant
Or meant to make amends? is generous or mean?

The casual word, the easiness, the quick straight answer,
The humane delay, the lack of cautiousness
That gave ample laughter to our evenings
Are too simple for these days of power
Whose nature is to hint not state.
So when one has a chance to talk the conversation
Hesitates on the brink of momentous things;
He ponders. . .
Suggesting by some unremark
There was much more to be said.

It's a pity: good men who seek to serve
Bind themselves unto a cause,
Then use the fate of nations as a rationale
To take their friends aside,
To lead themselves into some history.
We gain uncertain statesmen: many lose a friend.

But I am glad that others are powerful with compassion,
Who see before we do what troubles us
And help in kindness, take ignorance in tow.
If not for such we lose our gods
Who lived but now are dying in our friends.

Wendell Berry was born in Kentucky in 1934. He has authored more than 40 books, including eight novels (about the fictitious town of Port William) and more than two-dozen books of poetry. He has taught at universities including Stanford and the University of Kentucky, and is known for his environmental activism. He and his wife live on their farm in Port Royal, Kentucky.

The Way of Pain

1.
For parents, the only way
is hard. We who give life
give pain. There is no help.
Yet we who give pain
give love; by pain we learn
the extremity of love.

2.
I read of Abraham's sacrifice
the Voice required of him,
so that he led to the altar
and the knife his only son.
The beloved life was spared
that time, but not the pain.
It was the pain that was required.

3.
I read of Christ crucified,
the only begotten Son
sacrificed to flesh and time
and all our woe. He died
and rose, but who does not tremble
for his pain, his loneliness,
and the darkness of the sixth hour?
Unless we grieve like Mary
at His grave, giving Him up
as lost, no Easter morning comes.

4.

And then I slept, and dreamed
the life of my only son
was required of me, and I
must bring him to the edge
of pain, not knowing why.
I woke, and yet that pain
was true. It brought his life
to the full in me. I bore him
suffering, with love like the sun,
too bright, unsparing, whole.

The Peace of Wild Things

When despair for the world grows in me
and I wake in the night at the least sound
in fear of what my life and my children's lives may be,
I go and lie down where the wood drake
rests in his beauty on the water, and the great heron feeds.
I come into the peace of wild things
who do not tax their lives with forethought
of grief. I come into the presence of still water.
And I feel above me the day-blind stars
waiting with their light. For a time
I rest in the grace of the world, and am free.

The Wish to be Generous

 All that I serve will die, all my delights,
the flesh kindled from my flesh, garden and field,
the silent lilies standing in the woods,
the woods, the hill, the whole earth, all
will burn in man's evil, or dwindle

in its own age.
 Let the world bring on me
the sleep of darkness without stars, so I may know
my little light taken from me into the seed
of the beginning and the end, so I may bow
to mystery, and take my stand on the earth
like a tree in a field, passing without haste
or regret toward what will be, my life
a patient willing descent into the grass.

from **Sabbaths 1980 — I**

What hard travail God does in death!
He strives in sleep, in our despair,
And all flesh shudders underneath
The nightmare of His sepulcher.

The earth shakes, grinding its deep stone;
All night the cold wind heaves and pries;
Creation strains sinew and bone
Against the dark door where He lies.

The stem bent, pent in seed, grow straight
And stands. Pain breaks in song. Surprising
The merely dead, graves fill with light
Like opened eyes. He rests in rising.

from **Sabbaths 1999 — VI**

We travelers, walking to the sun can't see
Ahead, but looking back the very light
That blinded us shows us the way we came,
Along which blessings now appear, risen
As if from sightlessness to sight, and we,
By blessing brightly lit, keep going forward
That blessed light that yet to us is dark.

from **Sabbaths 1999 — IX**

The incarnate Word is with us,
is still speaking, is present
always, yet leaves no sign
but everything that is.

from **Sabbaths 2002 — X**

Teach me work that honors Thy work,
the true economies of goods and words,
to make my arts compatible
with the songs of the local birds.

Teach me patience beyond work
and, beyond patience, the blest
Sabbath of Thy unresting love
which lights all things and gives rest.

from **Sabbaths 2003 — IV**

The little stream sings
in the crease of the hill.
It is the water of life. It knows
nothing of death. nothing.
And this is the morning
of Christ's resurrection.
The tomb is empty. There is
no death. Death is our illusion,
our wish to belong only
to ourselves, which is our freedom
to kill one another.
From this sleep may we too
rise, as out of the dark grave.

Walt McDonald was born in Lubbock, Texas in 1934. He served in the U.S. Air Force, and is a veteran of Vietnam. In 1971 he founded the Creative Writing program at Texas Tech University. Among his more than twenty books, is *Faith is a Radical Master: New and Selected Poems* (Abilene Christian University Press, 2005). In 2001 he was named the first Poet Laureate of Texas.

Faith Is a Radical Master

We touch you one by one and mumble,
words stumbling on our tongues,
stunned in your blurred living room

hours after your lab report:
a little lump, a mass of bulged
malignant cells. Telephoned,

we've come to hold you. The ghost
who walked with mourners to Emmaus
may be in this room. We are mere mortals,

all. We don't know anything but this.
Who knows this winter drought will last?
Who swears the last blind beggar's

doomed, no spittle for his lids?
Who calls down fire from heaven
and isn't seared?

Settling the Plains

For here and for the afterlife
they worked and sang, kept time
with hymn books in both hands,
old songs of God's good grace

in a land so dry they planted
cottonseeds to prove they believed
in miracles. They buried their dead
on plains with no native stones,

deep in the earth to save them
from sandstorms that pounded
daily from the west. They prayed
for rain, the sun so dry for months

they couldn't curse. Rain fell
in floods like manna twice a year.
Like Moses, they walked across
dry land and called on God

to bless them all for doubting.
They believed whatever they put
in the dirt would live if it was
God's will and the wind blew.

Les Murray was born in 1938 in New South Wales. He is Australia's best known contemporary poet, and has won the T.S. Eliot Award and the Queen's Gold Medal for Poetry. He has published thirty books of poetry, including his *New Selected Poems* (Farrar Straus and Giroux, 2014), He also edited, *The Anthology of Australian Religious Poetry*.

Easter 1984

When we saw human dignity
healing humans in the middle of the day

we moved in on him slowly
under the incalculable gravity

of old freedom, of our own freedom,
under atmospheres of consequence, of justice

under which no one needs to thank anyone.
If this was God, we would get even.

And in the end we nailed him,
lashed, spittled, stretched him limb from limb.

We would settle with dignity
for the anguish it had caused us,

we'd send it to be abstract again,
we would set it free.

*****

But we had raised up evolution.
It would not stop being human.

Ever afterwards, the accumulation
of freedom would end in this man

whipped, bloodied, getting the treatment.
It would look like man himself getting it.

He was freeing us, painfully, from freedom,
justice, dignity — he was discharging them

of their deadly ambiguous deposit,
remaking out of them the primal day

in which he was free not to have borne it
and we were free not to have done it,

free never to torture man again,
free to believe him risen.

Poetry And Religion

Religions are poems. They concert
our daylight and dreaming mind, our
emotions, instinct, breath and native gesture

into the only whole thinking: poetry.
Nothing's said till it's dreamed out in words
and nothing's true that figures in words only.

A poem, compared with an arrayed religion,
may be like a soldier's one short marriage night
to die and live by. But that is a small religion.

Full religion is the large poem in loving repetition;
like any poem, it must be inexhaustible and complete
with turns where we ask Now why did the poet do that?

You can't pray a lie, said Huckleberry Finn;
you can't poe one either. It is the same mirror:

mobile, glancing, we call it poetry,

fixed centrally, we call it a religion,
and God is the poetry caught in any religion,
caught, not imprisoned. Caught as in a mirror

that he attracted, being in the world as poetry
is in the poem, a law against its closure.
There'll always be religion around while there is poetry

or a lack of it. Both are given, and intermittent,
as the action of those birds — crested pigeon, rosella parrot —
who fly with wings shut, then beating, and again shut.

The Knockdown Question

Why does God not spare the innocent?

The answer to that is not in
the same world as the question
so you would shrink from me
in terror if I could answer it.

The Poisons of Right and Left

for *Czeslaw Milosz*

You are what you have got
and: to love, you have to hate.
Two ideas that have killed and maimed
holocausts and myriads.

Tired from Understanding

Tired from understanding
life, the animals approach man
to be mystified.

Church

i.m. Joseph Brodsky

The wish to be right
has decamped in large numbers
but some come to God
in hopes of being wrong.

High on the end wall hangs
the Gospel, from before he was books.
All judging ends in his fix,
all, including his own.

He rose out of Jewish
not English evolution
and he said the lamp he held
aloft to all nations was Jewish.

Freedom still eats freedom,
justice eats justice, love —
even love. One retarded man said,
church makes me want to be naughty,

but naked in a muddy trench
with many thousands, someone's saying
the true god gives his flesh and blood.
Idols demand yours off you.

Jesus Was A Healer

Jesus was a healer
never turned a patient down
never charged coin or conversion
started off with dust and spittle
then re-tuned lives to pattern
simply by his attention
often surprised himself a little
by his unbounded ability
Jesus was a healer
reattached his captor's ear
opened senses, unjammed cripples
sent pigs to drown delirium
cured a shy tug at his hem
learned to transmit resurrection
could have stood more Thank You
for God's sake, which was his own
Jesus was a healer
keep this quiet, he would mutter
to his learners. Copy me
and they did to a degree
still depicted on church walls
cure without treatment or rehearsals.

Robert Siegel (1939—2012) directed the graduate Creative Writing program at the University of Wisconsin—Milwaukee for 23 years. His novels include the *Whalesong* trilogy, and his poetry includes his final book *Within This Tree of Bones: New and Selected Poems* (2013) from the Poiema Poetry Series. Siegel's poems often encounter the world from the perspective of an animal.

A Colt, the Foal of an Ass

Contemplating the dust he stands
in the direct unbearable noon, tethered
to the dead thorn. His long ears hang
down, twitch and revolve as a constant
small black cloud of flies
brassily land and bite and ascend. His hide
quivers at each bite and smoothes out
like this quake-tormented land,
while his bathrobe-tasseled tail larrups
and swats too late.
                        His eyes, half-lidded
in the bleaching light, are fixed and still;
his plain, dull face perpendicular as a post,
his forelock hanging over it.
                        He does not
turn toward the stranger who stands talking
with the two at the door. Only his muzzle,
soft as silk and still faintly pink,
twitches as his nostrils catch the foreign scent,
widen and lift his lip for half a second.
                                    Then
lazily he turns to look, eyes glazed, indifferent,
tugs at the harsh rope once, desists,
patient with donkey patience, already learning
the rough discipline that pulled him from the grass
and his mother's side.
                        Now, without warning,

as if he feels a tremor underfoot,
some inaudible alarm from the world's core,
he bares his teeth and breaks the air with a sound
like a stone wrenched and crying from its center,

harsh and grating as a rusty hinge
on which the whole earth hangs.

Later

there is a moment with a crowd roaring
in surges long and hoarse as breakers crashing,
cool green branches to tread over the hot stones,
and flowers which offer a brief fragrance under hoof—
one moment of all those in the years that are to come
of fetching and hauling for masters bad and good,
when he does not mind what he is carrying,
when a sense of joy returns like the early smell
of grass when he first stood, unsteady in the field,
with a beast's dim sense of liberty.

Still, he cannot guess what he is carrying
and will not remember this moment in all the years
until he is worn out, lame,
until the hammer is brought down on his unsuspecting head,
his hooves melted to glue, his hide thrown to the crows—
when he shall return to this now, this always,
he continues to live in,
this moment of bearing the man,
a weight that is light and easy,
celebrated in a rough, ecstatic chorus,
toward his own fatal burden heavier than the world.

9 A.M.

Yellow flames flutter
about the feeder:
a Pentecost of finches.

Ezekiel

Ezekiel saw the wheels within wheels.
His heart rose to his throat; a burning coal
purified both. The fear one usually feels
at such moments was gone. Transported, his soul

entered a quiet place, and while the creatures
moved without turning, he in his clear trance
noted their flight in detail, the particular features
of animal and angel moving in a dance

radiant as a rainbow. While there he heard
the awful message prophets usually bear,
before he saw in the valley of the bones
something more splendid than that which turned
in the heavens: dry bones grow whole and rise
and human flesh assume the immortal skies.

Judas

All along I was the only one who seemed to know
what the Man could do if he put his mind to it.
I'd seen him raise the dead, for God's sake, and control
the wind. Rome and her clackering legions would quit

Jerusalem tomorrow if he'd but say the word.
Or, if he wished it, thousands would die for him,
ecstatically falling upon the conqueror
with sticks and stones. So I waited for his least hint

of rebellion. But when he said he might choose
death, and how the Pharisees would see to that,
I couldn't believe him. Surely it was an elaborate ruse.
Surely at any armed threat he'd knock them flat!

He hinted as much to me, and I, conscious of the sin,
supped, betrayed, and kissed, that the battle might begin.

A Notable Failure

Holy Saturday

He never went abroad to broaden him
and though he learned to read, he did not write
anything worth saving. Once, at a whim,
he scribbled something they hadn't gotten right

in the sand and erased it. Few could know
whether to credit any of the vulgar rumors
surrounding his birth in a shed. There were low
whispers and a gap of thirty years.

Then more rumors trickled through the countryside
about the artisan's son turned wonderworker:
probably a charlatan—blasphemer to be sure. Wide-eyed,
some claimed he raised the dead (and healed *lepers!)*

before the Romans nailed him—as they nailed all such—
and the neighbors sniffed, "He didn't come to much!"

Thomas

The man was dead. I'd seen. And that was that.
I'd helped them bury him. The heart had stopped.
Later the women started in. Soon all were mad,
jabbering about seeing him, his wounds. They dropped

everything else and huddled to see a ghost
like the gentiles' squeaking wraiths and spooks.
At last I agreed to look but locked the door—no
tricks! Suddenly among them. . .I blinked and looked

twice—*He* was. "Thomas, put your finger here."
So I pressed the wounds—the hands, the side—
the flesh all torn pitifully. "My Lord, My God!"
Later He ate the fish and drank the wine

I handed him. I never took my eyes
off him, the living flesh, for which the starved heart cries.

Kelly Cherry was born in Baton Rouge, Louisiana, in 1940. She has written more than 20 books, including *Hazard and Prospect: New and Selected Poems* (LSU Press, 2007). Before retiring, she taught at the University of Wisconsin—Madison for more than 20 years. In 2010 she became the Poet Laureate of Virginia.

The Radical

Think of it: the master a servant.
Getting down on his knees,
washing the feet,
the Achilles' heels and calloused soles,
the secret, shamed places between the toes.

Not the symbolic swipe we see in the movies.
No, the towel getting filthier and filthier, after all the walking
they had done, and perhaps
the weather was not always so good
it had rained, there had been mud
it had not rained, it was extremely hot,
so hot they didn't even piss, residue of salt on their skin so thick
it was nearly geological,
as they crossed from Bethany into Jerusalem
and mixed in the crowded, urgent streets of the city,

which was palmy with spangled sunlight,
bright coins scattered on the buildings' sides.

So much yet to happen! And yet it would happen
and be over seemingly before it had begun,
the way life is,
the way we arrive at our single destination
before we have quite packed,
the bits and pieces of our experience exposed to anyone,
which means that the future is constantly revealing itself as having been
the past all along,

which means that time returns us to ourselves.

(Even if you thought you were moving away from yourself,
thought you could outpace that peculiar dialectic . . .)

And now he traces each instep with the nap of the towel
as if it were a country he wants to map,
as if he wants to remember where it has been,
the steps it took
to get here,
the earth it walked on—
to him, a miracle greater than walking on water.

Gethsemane

On a hill backlit by twilight,
the disciples gather like crows
for the night.
This is their down time, time to browse
among the olive branches, Christ with them,
their apostolic flight slowed at last to a head-nodding drowse,
to a flutter of tattered cloak, the unraveling hem
dragging in the dirt like a hurt wing.
They flock momentarily around him,
then settle down, safe in the soft swing
of wind that rises and then falls back
with the deepening evening
into the distance, and sleep, while Christ's black
feathers burn in his father's fist,
plucked by God before by Judas kissed.

Golgotha

They were scattered on the hillside like stones,
polished by the wind-rag: the smooth, shining bones,
cheekbone and eye socket, the empty skull-cases

of brains that had vanished into various gullets, leaving no traces
of thought, not even a single, stray
idea. For much of that long, painful day

he must have contemplated the meanings of
erosion, mortal decay, vanity, impermanence, rather than love,
until in the lengthening light

that drew on toward—but he would never see it—that night,
he saw—a trick of his blood-blurred eyes, perhaps—them move,
and knew the meaning of the skulls was love

and the one proposition needing no proof
is that God exists because God thinks or is thought of.
God is what remains in the final analysis.

Paul Mariani was born in 1940 in New York City. He is University Professor of English at Boston College, and writes in the mode of fellow confessional poets. His seventh poetry collection is *Epitaphs for the Journey: New, Selected and Revised Poems* (2012) from the Poiema Poetry Series. He has also written biographies of the poets William Carlos Williams, John Berryman, Robert Lowell, Hart Crane and Gerard Manley Hopkins.

Death & Transfiguration

Down the precipitous switchbacks at eighty
the pokerfaced Palestinian cabby aims his Mercedes
while the three of us, ersatz pilgrims, blank-eyed, lurch,
and the droll Franciscan goes on about the Art Deco Church

of the Transfiguration crowning the summit of the Mount.
Up there I'd touched the damp stones of the old Crusader fount,
paced the thick walls, imagined Muslims circling below
on horseback, muleback, then ascending for the final blow.

A decent pasta and a dry wine, thanks to the Fratelli who run
the hostel at the site, followed by an even drier lecture in the sun-
drenched court, then back down to the glinting taxis, ready
to return us now to the same old, feverish, unsteady

world half a mile below. I thought of the old masters, so
many of them who had tried to ignite this scene—Angelico,
di Buoninsegna, Bellini, Perugino, the Frenchman John of Berry,
the Preobrazheniye (Russian, Novgorod, sixteenth century)—

and thought at last of what Raphael had wrought. It was to be
his final work, commissioned for some French cathedral, his early
death at thirty-seven intervening. For those who only dream
of some vertiginous, longed-for transfiguration, he would seem

to hold out something magnanimous and large: the benzene brightness
of the Christ, eyes upraised in the atom flash of whiteness,

that body lifted up, cloud-suspended feet above the earth. There,
on either side, with the Tablets and the Book: Moses and Elijah.

Below, his fear-bedazzled friends: Peter, James and John. And though
paint is only paint, we can almost hear the Father's words again, so
caught up in the vision was the artist: *This is my beloved Son,
on whom my favor rests. Listen to him.* Meanwhile, someone

in the lower half of the picture is gesturing toward the transfigured
Christ. He is part of the curious and anxious crowd
that surrounds the epileptic youth, whose eyes, like Christ's, are wide,
but wide with seizure like some frenzied Sibyl's: the great divide

that separates him from the others, as if he understood the same
strange
thing Raphael came to see as he composed this scene: that the
deranged
youth has somehow come upon a mystery. Like us, he has been bound
round with fear, and only the One descending as he comes can sound

those depths of cosmic light and dark, in which the young man
writhes honeystuck in death, though he will—the gospel says—be
raised again
to health and to his father, in this prologue to the resurrection.
That's it, then, it would seem: first the old fears descending, then
dejection

and the dunning sameness in the daily going round and round of
things.
Then a light like ten thousand suns that flames the brain and brings
another kind of death with it, and then—once more—the daily round
again. But changed now by what the blind beseeching eye has found.

The Passage

So I opened the little book she'd placed
there on the table and half shouted since
she didn't have her hearing aids plugged in,
reading aloud the passage she'd pointed to,
the one about prayer sometimes being all
you have to link you to your loved ones,
especially where death or distance come
between. She turned to her husband
of sixty years, still working over his bowl
of bran flakes. Did you hear that, Phil,
she said, to which my father-in-law,
half-startled, bobbed his head, yes, yes,
though probably he hadn't. Then she turned
to me, eyes burning with the bituminous
shine of a girl of twenty.
                                    I have known
this woman now for forty years,
yet never once saw her search my face
like this, with the beseeching gaze of
a baby robin waiting to be fed. Besides,
she was fast approaching the threshold
now of some great mystery. She wanted
to be fed and I had fed her as
I could, with the words I witnessed
turn to bread before us on the table.

Nine One One

Once again the nightmare. The blue-black plume,
The billowing flame. All my life I've been afraid
Of tall buildings, and here was the tallest, down
Near Manhattan's prow. Firemen and police officers
Kept running *towards* the flames! People were falling
Or jumping. No one yet seemed to understand
What was happening. How will they put it out,
I kept wondering. Then the second tower.
Then the Pentagon. Then a fourth jet, down

Somewhere over Pennsylvania. Reality itself
Seemed to buckle with the buckling towers.
"Mourn for the city," a man who knew
His Apocalypse quoted me later that week.
The Scarlet City, he said. All over again. Gone.
Gone in an hour. But who deserved this? These
Were folks with families, folks with mortgages
To pay. You or me in the right place
At the wrong time. Plans put on hold. Forever.

Nurses waiting for patients who never appeared.
A priest saying Mass in the smouldering rubble.
The dead, the many dead, and the millions more
Wounded that morning. Mother of sorrows,
What can I say? Here in my room, I watch you
Watching your son, the one they will crucify
In their own good time, as they crucified him here
At Ground Zero. A mother grieves, while
Her little ones wonder where is their daddy.

And where *are* the lost who paid with their lives?
A mother grieves, and my eye follows hers down
To her child. Remember, he says at the omega point
Of the final Book, Remember this well. I am
The morning star rising once more above

My beloved city, as above the homes of my Afghans,
Above my whole bent, broken world. Have I not
Told you I will not leave you orphans? Not
One of you. Not one, not a single precious one.

Annunciation

Three birds sang from the shaded grove.
The lilies shook and nodded, the white stones shone.
Through every leaf the dazzle of blue light,
and clouds chevying eastward out to sea.
And now. . .now, the pregnant silence of your word.
This is the moment I have waited for all week
as I have prayed here pleading for your peace.
Once, among the stalls at Marrakech, one man
looped a freighted snake about my son's bare neck,
while another shook a basket in my startled eyes.
He was grinning as he circled me, while I
threw whatever money I had at them,
begging them to take the thing away. And now,
like that, so quietly, a sudden breeze comes up
to kiss me on my forehead, the way a mother will,
when she sighs goodnight, goodnight, and covers you,
her sandal's heel firmly on the writhing serpent's head.

The Sick Man

He was coming back it was a long way yet
and the narrow passage was dark
but there was a light dim and hovering ahead
he knew what being on the edge of life
was like now and he wanted life wanted
breath air light love he was not
very coherent yet that much he knew
but he wanted to think more clearly
to behold once more the blossoms
on the ancient catalpa in his yard
as they fell in the breeze like
a gentle snow and pick the white
orchid-shaped things up by the handful
and rub their grapey perfume gently
against his nose and breathe in the sweet
earth again and again and please God again

B.H. Fairchild was born in Houston in 1942. He received the National Book Critics Circle Award for *Early Occult Memory Systems of the Lower Midwest* (2004). He is a professor of English at the University of North Texas. His latest book is *The Blue Buick: Selected and New Poems* (W.W. Norton/2016).

The Problem

The name of the bow is life, but its work is death.

–The Fragments

How in Heraclitus
ideas of things, quality, and event
coalesce—sun/warmth/dawn—
the perceiver/perceived, too,
not yet parsed, not yet,
and then the great Forgetting,
breath and breather, love and beloved,
world and God-in-the-world.
But then it comes upon us: that brightness,
that bright tension in animals, for instance,
that focus, that compass
of the mammalian mind finding
its own true North,
saintly in its dark-eyed,
arrow-eared devotion.
A kind of calling, a via negativa,
a surrender, still and silent, to the heart's desire.
So in the cathedral of the world
we hold communion,
the bread of language
placed delicately upon our tongues
as we breathe the bitter air,
drinking the wine of reason
and pressing to our breasts the old dream of Being.

The Deposition

And one without a name
Lay clean and naked there, and gave commandments.

—Rilke, "Washing the Corpse"
(trans. Jarrell)

Dust storm, we thought, a brown swarm
plugging the lungs, or a locust-cloud,
but this was a collapse, a slow sinking
to deeper brown, and deeper still, like the sky
seen from inside a well as we are lowered down,
and the air twisting and tearing at itself.
But it was done. And the body hung there
like a butchered thing, naked and alone
in a sudden hush among the ravaged air.
The ankles first—slender, blood-caked,
pale in the sullen dark, legs broken
below the knees, blue bruises smoldering
to black. And the spikes. We tugged iron
from human flesh that dangled like limbs
not fully hacked from trees, nudged
the cross beam from side to side until
the sign that mocked him broke loose.
It took all three of us. We shouldered the body
to the ground, yanked nails from wrists
more delicate, it seemed, than a young girl's
but now swollen, gnarled, black as burnt twigs.
The body, so heavy for such a small man,
was a knot of muscle, a batch of cuts
and scratches from the scourging, and down
the right side a clotted line of blood,
the sour posca clogging his ragged beard,
the eyes exploded to a stare that shot
through all of us and still speaks in my dreams:
I know who you are.

So, we began to wash
the body, wrenching the arms, now stiff
and twisted, to his sides, unbending
the ruined legs and sponging off the dirt
of the city, sweat, urine, shit—all the body
gives—from the body, laying it out straight
on a sheet of linen rank with perfumes
so that we could cradle it, haul it
to the tomb. The wind shouted.
The foul air thickened. I reached over
to close the eyes. I know who you are.

Sydney Lea was born near Philadelphia in 1942. He has taught at Middlebury College and many other colleges, and was the founding editor of *New England Review*. He has published twelve poetry collections—including *Six Sundays Toward a Seventh* (2012), which is the first book in the Poiema Poetry Series. From 2011 to 2015 he was Poet Laureate of Vermont.

Barnet Hill Brook

Here's what to read in mud by the brook after last night's storm,
Which inscribed itself on sky as light, now here, now gone—

And matchless. I kneel in the mud, by scrimshaw of rodents, by twinned
Neat stabs of weasel. I won't speak of those flashes. Here by my hand,

The lissome trail of a worm that lies nearby under brush,
Carnal pink tail showing out. Gnats have thronged my face.

I choose not to fend them off. Except for my chest in its slight
Lifting and sinking, the place's stillness feels complete.

Its fullness too: in the pool above the dead grass dam,
The water striders are water striders up and down:

They stand on themselves, feet balanced on feet in mirroring water.
How many grains of sand in the world? So one of my daughters

Wanted to know in her little girlhood. "Trillions," I said.
"I love you," she answered back. "I love you more than that."

Lord knows I'm not a man who deserves to be so blessed.
I choose to believe that there's grace, that the splendid universe

Lies not in my sight but subsumes my seeing, my small drab witness.
Tonight my eye may look on cavalcades of brightness,

Of star and planet. Or cloud again. And when I consider,
O, what is man, That thou art mindful of him, it's proper

For me to have knelt, if only by habit. Pine needles let go,
And drop, and sink to this rillet's bright white bottomstones.

To tally them up would take me a lifetime. And more would keep
coming.
A lifetime at least. And more would keep coming, please God, keep
coming.

I Was Thinking of Beauty

– for Gregory Wolfe

I've surrendered myself to Mingus's *Tijuana Moods*
on my obsolete record machine, sitting quiet as I sat last night.
I was thinking of beauty then, how it's faced grief since the day
that somebody named it. Plato; Aquinas; the grim rock tablets
that were handed down to Moses by Yahweh, with His famous stricture
on the graven image. Last evening, I was there when some noted
professor

in a campus town to southward addressed what he called, precisely,
The Issue of Beauty. Here was a person who seemed to believe
his learned jargon might help the poor because his lecture
would help to end the *exploitations of capitalism* —
which pays his wage at the ivied college through which he leads
the impressionable young, soon to be managers, brokers, bankers.

He was hard above all on poems, though after a brief appearance
poetry seemed to vanish. It was gone before I knew it.
The professor quoted, *Beauty is Truth, Truth Beauty,* then chuckled.
He explained that such a claim led to loathsome politics.
I'm afraid he lost me. Outside, the incandescent snow
of February sifted through the quad's tall elm trees,

hypnotic. Tonight as I sit alone and listen, the trumpet
on *Tijuana Gift Shop* lurches my heart wih its syncopations.
That's the rare Clarence Shaw, who vanished one day, though Mingus heard
he was teaching hypnosis somewhere. But back again to last evening:
I got thinking of Keats composing and coughing, of Abby Lincoln,
of Lorrain and Petrarch, of Callas and Isaac Stern. I was lost

in memory and delight, terms without doubt nostalgic.
I summoned a dead logger friend's description of cedar waxwings
on the bright mountain ash outside his door come middle autumn.
I remembered how Earl at ninety had called those verdigris birds
well groomed little folks. Which wasn't eloquent, no,
but passion showed in the way Earl waved his workworn hands

as he thought of beauty, which, according to our guest,
was opiate. Perhaps. And yet I went on for no reason
to consider Maori tattoos: elaborate and splendid,
Trinidadians shaping Big Oil's rusty abandoned barrels
to play on with makeshift mallets, toxic junk turning tuneful.
The poor you have always with you, said an even more famous speaker,

supreme narcotic dealer no doubt in our speaker's eyes —
eyes that must never once have paused to behold a bird,
ears that deafened themselves to the song of that bird or any.
Beauty's a drug, he insisted, from which we must wean the poor,
indeed must wean ourselves. But I was thinking of beauty
as something that will return — here's Curtis Porter's sweet horn —

outlasting our disputations. I was thinking it never had gone.

The Pastor

I have just one person left on earth who's been
My friend through grade school, high school, church, and sports,
The pastor says. Meanwhile the winter rain
Explodes on the metal roof like handgun shots,

And it's hard to hear the man go on: *Thing is,*
He's lost his memory. There comes a catch
In his throat, a thing that no one here has witnessed
Through all his ministry. *Here's the trouble*, he adds,

I'm left alone with the things we knew together.
Silence ensues, save for a few quiet coughs,
And rustlings of the worship programs' paper.
Then the preacher seems to change his theme right off,

Speaking of Mary, and how she must have suffered
When her son referred to his apostolic peers
As family, not to her or his brothers,
Not to Joseph—as if he forgot the years

Spent in their household, as if he kept no thought
Of ties that bind. The congregants are old.
They try to listen, but their minds go wandering off
To things like the pounding rain outside, so cold

And ugly and loud. The storm, so out of season,
So wintry, still improbably recalls
The milder months, which vanished in a moment,
And which they summon vaguely, if at all.

Through a Window

I read a poem each Sunday   Our pastor calls this *Ministry*
of Verse   I try to find a poem not just she but anyone
will get   A short poem if I can for fear someone like Timmy
who isn't all that into poems to begin with may complain

I try to select some lines that represent what I believe
and more or less what the people there believe   I have friends too
outside the church who cannot believe that I in fact believe
say in miracles   They ask can you really believe they're true

exactly   Poems cannot be exact   I'm thinking how I'll sound
My vanity lives on   I don't read my poems which grow shorter
as I grow old   I once imagined I must go on and on
to get at things I thought I knew but I know more than ever

I know nothing now   No my friends I don't believe exactly
in miracles   I believe inexactly   I see Mary
Magdalene just for instance in that garden quite unclearly
Still I see her   I see Tess as well who's married to Timmy

and seems confused   Well she *is* confused   Dementia has her down
Her husband's there   He holds her hand   Timmy holds things
together
I've thought at times like anybody I couldn't hold my own
yet I'm alive   I hear a bird sing one small massive wonder

John F. Deane was born in 1943 on Ireland's Achill Island. He is the author of many poetry collections, including *Snow Falling On Chestnut Hill: New and Selected Poems* (Carcanet, 2012). More than thirty years ago he founded *Poetry Ireland Review*, and Dedalus Press. His *Give Dust A Tongue: A Faith Memoir* appeared in 2015 (Columba Press).

Officium

Spare me Lord for my days burn off like dew.
What is man that you should magnify him;
why do you tender towards him your heart of love?
You visit him at dawn, touching him with dreams,
whisper to him at dusk, while the swings still shift
and soft rain falls on the abandoned frames.
Why have you made him contrary to you
that he learn baseness, anger and defeat
swallowing his own saliva in sudden dread?
Can you erase his sins, like chalk-marks,
or place your angels as a fence about him?
The trees dreep softly, the attendants are gone home.
Today I will lie down in sand, and if tomorrow
you come in search of me, I am no more.

Fantasy In White

Over the brimming acres of wild meadow
the white butterflies, in a silent storm
of winged snowflakes, were fluttering
through their extravagant mating dance;
in this our fractured time and world-space
those of us who know ourselves to be broken
rejoiced in a moment of purest wonder;
where sin abounds there grace abounds the more.
By evening, absence had settled on the meadow

as after the exhalation of a deep-drawn breath,
one high star chilling in a grey, bleak sky;
imperceptibly the fall had come
and we turned once more towards the dark,
the white soul weighted in its winter boots.

Viola d'Amore

I had been playing Bach on the great organ —
"A Mighty Fortress is our God" —
the church below me empty in the nowhere afternoon
bombarde, clarion, celeste

and when I lifted fingers from the keys
it was, for a moment, eternity and the walls of the world
contained nothing but the lingering breath of the harmony,

rafters of the loft had lifted while the whole sky
trembled in a breeze that rippled slow across it
till all I knew was the touch of the fingers of Jesus

soft on my fingertips, my body
consciously drawing breath, my bones
refusing their earthy weight, and my soul
ringing with immortality.

Night Prayer

Rembrandt: Landscape with the Rest on the Flight into Egypt

I

This, too, you see, is prayer, these words I labour to admit
   under the spirit's prompting, words on the notebook
   difficult to decipher, the ink flowing out too fast

in the first stirrings; pen, copybook and keyboard
   in an attempt to touch the source of light,
   of life, the groundwork of our hope. Here, too,

II

figures in a nightscape, a pause in the difficult journey; questions
   of resting in penumbra, of knowing light is fragile,
   like a child holding its greedy mouth to the breast;

there is a fire of sticks, trouvaille of twig and branch, to keep
   wolves at bay (between here and destination, Emmaus, say,
   beyond a life's full circle, light against the darkness) and this

III

is Jesus, name and nature of our source and sustenance, this
   is God, dwarfed by trees and distances, enormous landscape
   and a darkening night, and you grow aware that here

the watchful small lamps of greed and power are looming over all.
   The canvas, too, is prayer, impasto, brush and palette knife,
   working to ease the blackness about the light, cognisant

IV

of the death of innocents; it is all self-portrait, still life, a halt
   in the hastening, the helplessness of humankind before its own,
   the helplessness of God trusting Himself to flesh;

love is a small child, far from consciousness, hunted; should he be

found and killed, what then? what then? Rembrandt
knew that distance between himself and God – all time, all space, all

V

life, all death – had been too great; the instruments of art, sharpened
and
    softened in the desiring heart, shorten the distance, finding
    a sheltering tree, light shouldering the darkness; this

Egypt of the imagination, this den of safety called
    exile, as world with its instruments of power and economics
    preys on you and how can you believe your pigments

VI

touch beyond impossibility? Image, less real than
    thistledown in a western gale, less permanent than golden light
    reflected on a pond, you try to empty the ocean of silence

with the holding power of pigments, the silence that is God.
    Christ-beyond-all-grasping, the heart in its pleading is a series
    of shifting darkscapes, vaulted in night-prayer passageways.

Name and Nature

Your name, Jesus, is childhood in the body, at times
a single malt upon the tongue, Vivaldi to the ears;

your name, Christ, forgiveness to the heart, acceptance
to the flesh, a troubled joy across the soul;

at ever my very best I will plead to you, closest to me,
for kindness. Perhaps the silence I take for God's

non-presence is the noise in which I have immersed
my life; nor have I framed a quiet to correspond

to his, where I might find my every call
answered. I seek kind. You are the reality I cling to,

the flesh, the history, the spurting out of blood. I believe
the non-attendance of my God lies in my absence from him

and he is present, like the embrace of air
or the inward forces of the seasons. Your name, Jesus,

is the river on which I float, your name, Christ, the ocean
where everything is in place, is shivering, beautiful, and apart.

John Leax was born in 1943. He served as Professor of English and Poet-in-residence at Houghton College in upstate New York from 1969 to 2009. Jack experiments with his verse, often having a significantly different tone from one book to another. Recent collections include *Recluse Freedom* (WordFarm, 2012) and *Remembering Jesus: Sonnets and Songs* (Poiema Poetry Series, 2014).

At the Winter Feeder

His feather flame doused dull
by icy cold,
the cardinal hunched
into the rough, green feeder
but ate no seed.
Through binoculars I saw
festered and useless
his beak, broken
at the root.
Then two: one blazing, one gray,
rode the swirling weather
into my vision
and lighted at his side.
Unhurried, as if possessing
the patience of God,
they cracked sunflowers
and fed him
beak to wounded beak
choice meats.
Each morning and afternoon
the winter long,
that odd triumvirate,
that trinity of need,
returned and ate
their sacrament
of broken seed.

Faith in a Seed

And now, late summer, the young
robins marching about
displaying speckled breasts
and fierce dispositions,
the starlings spaced evenly
along the power lines anticipating
the rush of arctic winds,
the goldfinch males, brilliant
in their patience, mounting the purple
sumac and calling their olive mates
to love, for now is seedtime.
The flowers, spent, spend all
their wealth to buy another season
from the cold, and the finches,
nesting late and well, find
in the wild dispersion
the satisfaction of every want
they neither know nor question.

Old Shepherd

Luke 2:13–14

As winter cold leans hard upon my back,
 I long for once-upon-a-time when I
Was small enough my elders watched the black
Night through and let me sleep. Only the cry
Of the ewe in lambing time caused them to make
Me rise; my hands were small to ease a birth.
I minded them and rose. This night I shake
Beside the fire. Wind blowing from the north,
 Disturbs the boy I used to be. No stars
Blanket his sleep. Once to voices brilliant

In light I woke. We found a child not far
From where we kept our sheep. Rough celebrants,
We woke his mother from her careful rest.
Like a lamb newborn he nestled at her breast.

Daughter

Luke 8: 49–56

I don't remember. I was twelve, not yet
Aware of how a parent dies before
A child's bewilderment. I lay beset
By fever, lost to life. I will not bore
You reconstructing how they called my name
And wept. They were, perhaps, more deeply stricken
Than some, my father's leadership a claim
On God's beneficence. I've forgotten—
I don't remember anger. No. What stays
With me is waking to voices about
My bed, one voice clear in the haze
Of wonder, and my father's joyous shout.

 So long ago now! I live bound by that surprise
And long to hear again that voice, "Daughter, arise."

A Woman of the City

Luke 7:36–39

How the alabaster jar of ointment came
Into my hands is a story mothers tell
To sons they love, as if dull words could tame
The urge that rings in flesh like death's sweet knell.
Forget that. Begin with me weeping, crouched
At the teacher's feet, road-calloused, dirt-caked,
Unwashed by the preening Pharisee slouched
Satisfied at the table. My tears snaked
Down my Savior's instep. My unbound hair
Fell loosely and dried the kisses I'd
Lavished with the ointment. I was all need. The air
Swirled with perfume as if a king had died.
My touch moved him! I felt his life quicken!
One word made me his forever—*forgiven.*

The High Priest's Maid

Mark 14:66–70

The courtyard fire collapsed, its light falling
Into itself, its warmth withdrawing from
The night. I laid fresh thorn on it, stalling
The creep of cold against the coming kingdom.

One stood nearby, obscured in cloaking shadows.
In the quick flare of the thorn I knew his face:
"You are with Jesus?" I asked. He swore, "God knows,
I'm not." And he was not—except by grace.

Nor then was I; the rope of lawless dread that bound
Christ's friend bound me. He fled, a mutineer,

93

Sinking in the night as once he nearly drowned,
His drifting eyes turned inward on his fear.

The Spirit lifted him at Pentecost:
His fiery word retrieved me from the lost.

Prayer

Matthew 26:25, 27:5

I dream of grace. The tongue that might have praised,
That might have sung forgiveness equal to
The sum of all the mercy God shot through
Creation when his stone-sealed Son blazed
Awake, the light to light betrayal's dark
Design, is swollen black in the hole that was
A mouth; my brother, Judas, hanged the ark
Of his redemption. Still I dream of grace.
I dream I take him from his tree, and lift
Him up to life. Should one betrayal cost
A soul—eternity demand such thrift
Of grace—the lost remain forever lost?

How then my three denials be forgiven?
Christ, Savior, win your chosen back for Eden.

Mother

Luke 23:42–43

Bitter my name should be. My mother's watch
Beneath the cross, my son hanging in day
Light dark, endures. No moment in a notch
Of passing time, I walk there now. It is my way.
Hope holds me yet in that hour when I heard
My son, whose voice could bring sullen people
To the edge of insurrection, find the Word
Till now unknown. Nailed to his grim pole,
He rounded to the truth. "Jesus, when you come
Into your kingdom," he begged, "remember me."
Christ turned as still he turns when hearts plumb
True and spoke, "Today with me you will be
In Paradise." The Word addressed my son!
My grief! My grief enthrones God's Holy One.

Jeanne Murray Walker was born in Minnesota in 1944. Her eighth poetry collection is *Helping the Morning: New and Selected Poems* (WordFarm, 2014). Her plays have also been widely performed. She heads the creative writing program at The University of Delaware where she has been a Professor of English for forty years.

In the Beginning Was the Word

It was your hunch, this world. On the heyday
of creation, you called, *Okay, go*! and a ball
of white hot gasses spun its lonely way
for millions of years, all spill and dangerous fall
until it settled into orbit. And a tough
neighborhood, it was, too. Irate Mars,
and sexually explicit Venus, the kerfluff
of a moody moon, and self-important stars.

And trees. Think of their endless rummage
for light, their photo-what's-it, how their growing
is barely regulated damage. Then birds,
mice, sheep. Soon people, bursting into language.
Creation thinking about itself: our words soaring
like yours through time, dangerous, ordinary words.

Leaving the Planetarium

*"Old things are passed away; behold, all
things are become new."*

—2 Corinthians 5:17 (KJV)

You pull at my sweater, weeping,
and I lift you from your seat.
We stumble out together. It's too much
for a five-year-old, too much red
fire raining down. Years from now,
long after your great-great-grandchildren are dead,
the sun, having burned its own body up,
will reach out like a jealous father
to eat his children—Mercury, first, then Venus.
The next day there will be a last
perfect sunrise, and afterwards,
an arm of fire will embrace
the one Earth
you think you cannot do without.
But I tell you,
my tiny flash of light,
you will be blazing like a sun by then,
and everyone you care for
will have swum into sharper focus,
like a picture that's developed slowly.
By then we will remember the Earth
only as the place where, long ago,
we first learned how to love.

—For Jack

Bergman

I am at the movies, practicing the discipline
of the sane, taking the characters
to my heart, while reminding myself
they're not me. Red scarf flying against snow
like a flag of happiness. Their looks meeting
across a table in the café. That blessing of first love,
to have your gaze returned. Then later,
the misunderstanding, that bewildering
shift. His face looming big as a baseball field,
his eyebrows flying like hysterical seagulls.
He has just begun to shout when the film gets stuck,

the same ugly word, ugly word he can't call back,
a word she can't forgive. In the booth
a kid bends over the projector,
a god now, performing small maneuvers of love
as we stare at the palpitating hooha
of the man's mouth, the cruelty in her eyes,

watching how habit can harden the heart, how
it's possible to cross into a country beyond choice,
beyond remorse, beyond forgiveness,
how even Pharoah didn't know exactly when,
between the first and tenth plagues,
he found himself inside the answer he could never
change, the way we are stuck in the film's reiterating

stutter. Until the boy cuts it. We go home early.
I turn the key in the lock, hearing the wind in the trees,
the sound of God weeping, His heart shattered on
the stubborn mystery of the human will.

Miniature Psalm of Complaint

You claim you've weighed the mountains
in your scales. But have you noticed smaller

chunks of the world are flaking off?
I sweep leaves from the walk. The oak,

like the mainmast of a warship, towers
above me, sending down its brown hands,

which hardly weigh a thing. So many friends
sick now. As for me? A bit of bone and hair.

My arteries ordinary as the pipes and spigots
that bring us water. Your thunder shakes my teeth.

On our hillside, your fingers of drizzle pick the final
chrysanthemums to pieces. I don't bear a grudge,

mind you, only wonder if you would step closer,
say something smaller. Back in the house,

wiping my feet, I hear a scratching. A dentist
with his pick. Or maybe a mouse. Two brilliant eyes,

cowlicky fur, in her genetic coding, years
of wiles. As she helps herself to our birdseed,

I hear her tiny breathing. Okay, I think,
okay. What she is, can't help, didn't ask for,

and is doomed to love—herself. I flick on
the porch light to keep her safe from owls.

I can almost see us from the road, our tiny house,
hanging like one last gold leaf in the oak tree.

Staying Power

*In appreciation of Maxim Gorky at the International
Convention of Atheists. 1929*

Like Gorky, I sometimes follow my doubts
outside and question the metal sky,
longing to have the fight settled, thinking
I can't go on like this, and finally I say

all right, it is improbable, all right, there
is no God. And then as if I'm focusing
a magnifying glass on dry leaves, God blazes up.
It's the attention, maybe, to what isn't

there that makes the notion flare like
a forest fire until I have to spend the afternoon
dragging the hose to put it out. Even
on an ordinary day when a friend calls,

tells me they've found melanoma,
complains that the hospital is cold, I say God.
God, I say as my heart turns inside out.
Pick up any language by the scruff of its neck,

wipe its face, set it down on the lawn,
and I bet it will toddle right into the godfire
again, which—though they say it doesn't
exist—can send you straight to the burn unit.

Oh, we have only so many words to think with.
Say God's not fire, say anything, say God's
a phone, maybe. You know you didn't order a phone,
but there it is. It rings. You don't know who it could be.

You don't want to talk, so you pull out
the plug. It rings. You smash it with a hammer

till it bleeds springs and coils and clobbered up
metal bits. It rings again. You pick it up

and a voice you love whispers hello.

Barbara Crooker was born in 1945 in New York State, and presently lives in Pennsylvania. Her six poetry collections include *Gold* (Poiema Poetry Series, 2013), and her *Selected Poems* (FutureCycle, 2015). She has received may honors, including the 2003 Thomas Merton Poetry of the Sacred Award.

All That Is Glorious Around Us

is not, for me, these grand vistas, sublime peaks, mist-filled
overlooks, towering clouds, but doing errands on a day
of driving rain, staying dry inside the silver skin of the car,
160,000 miles, still running just fine. Or later,
sitting in a café warmed by the steam
from white chicken chili, two cups of dark coffee,
watching the red and gold leaves race down the street,
confetti from autumn's bright parade. And I think
of how my mother struggles to breathe, how few good days
she has now, how we never think about the glories
of breath, oxygen cascading down our throats to the lungs,
simple as the journey of water over a rock. *It is the nature*
of stone / to be satisfied / writes Mary Oliver, *It is the nature*
of water / to want to be somewhere else, rushing down
a rocky tor or high escarpment, the panoramic landscape
boundless behind it. But everything glorious is around
us already: black and blue graffiti shining in the rain's
bright glaze, the small rainbows of oil on the pavement,
where the last car to park has left its mark on the glistening
street, this radiant world.

On Reading Charles Wright on a Fall Afternoon

sitting in an Adirondack chair, paint peeled mostly off, just the
    pentimento
of green. . . . Not a cloud anywhere; the pure blue verb of the sky.
The sun slants down, limitless, even as I'm feeling my days,
and how they are numbered, wondering how many more autumns
I've got in the bank, how many words are left in the pen. . . .
In this post-modern world we are not supposed to talk of the presence
of God, but I know after surgery, someone came into the room,
invisible, and held my hand. No birds are singing or flitting from bush
    to tree;
even the lawn seems to have given up, exhausted, exhaled its last green
    breath.
The dead come back, but they no longer speak our language. Ring me
    like a bell
in this brassy sunlight; wash me clean. Speak in the tongues of flowers.
The kudzu is covering the trees; they bend, but do not break.

Late Prayer

It's not that I'm not trying
to love the world and everything
in it, but look, that includes people
who shoot up schools, not just the blue
bird in his coat of sky, his red & white vest,
or the starry asters speckling the field—
It has to include talk show hosts
and all their blather, men with closed
minds and hard hearts, not only this sky,
full of clouds as a field of sheep,
or this wind, pregnant with rain. Don't
I have enough in my life; what is this
wild longing? Is there more to this world
than the shining surfaces? Will I be strong

103

enough to row across the ocean of loss
when my turn comes to take the oars?

The Book of Kells: Chi Rho

The work, not of men, but of angels.   Gerald of Wales

With quills and ink of iron gall on folded vellum,
monks in their cells labored in hives of stone,
producing pages that glistened like honey,
sweetening the word of God. On this page, the chi
commands the eye, its arm swooping to the left
in an elegant scrawl, the smaller rho and iota
nestled to the right. Knotwork fills each letter
to the brim. Three angels fly from the crossed
arms, heaven and earth intertwined, coiled spirals
connected by curves. Despite the gleam, no gold
is used, just layers of color built up like enamel.
In the interstices, creatures of air: birds and moths;
creatures of sea: fish and otters; creatures of land:
cats and mice. For the whole world was holy,
not just parts of it. The world was the Book of God.
The alphabet shimmered and buzzed with beauty.

Passerines

The last two lines are from Isaiah 55

This had been a difficult week, us at cross purposes,
spring lagging behind, dragging its feet, and days
on end of steady rain. The calendar said *t-shirts,*
flip flops, sandals, but we were hunched in sweaters,
stoking the fire. And then, and I know it was not
a miracle, the rain lifted, and the grass was a jolt
of electric green. The quarrel we were nursing
evaporated like morning mist, and there,
at the feeder, after years of trying—making
nectar, slicing oranges—was a pair of orioles, startling
as if the sun decided to fly down from the sky,
a flashy splash of citrus soda in my ordinary backyard.
Come all you who are thirsty, come to the waters.
You will go out in joy and be led forth in peace.

Sanctus

A goldfinch, bright as a grace note, has landed
on a branch across the creek that mutters and murmurs
to itself as it rushes on, always in a hurry.
The *ee oh lay* of a wood thrush echoes from deep
in the forest, someplace green. In paintings,
the Holy Ghost usually takes the form of a stylized
dove, its whiteness a blaze of purity. But what if
it's really a mourning dove, ordinary as daylight
in its old coat, nothing you'd ever notice.
When he rises from the creek and the light flares
behind, his tail is edged in white scallops,
shining. And when he opens his beak,
isn't he calling your name,
sweet and low, You, you, you?

Marilyn Nelson was born in Cleveland in 1946. Her books *The Fields of Praise: New and Selected* Poems (1997) and *Faster Than Light: New and Selected Poems* 1996–2011 (2012) are published by LSU Press. She served as Poet Laureate of Connecticut from 2001 to 2006. She is Professor Emeritus of English at the University of Connecticut.

from **Thus Far By Faith**

III. Sermon in the Ruined Garden
James 2:14–18

A mule meanders into sunshine from the wood
near Sally's garden. Almost nothing left
after the locust tides of the bereft
swept north. Some die for truth; some died for food.
Uncle Warren plucks a few choice stalks of grass,
chirrups and holds it in an outstretched hand.
The mule flinches just out of reach, to stand
flat-eared, tail flickering, willful as an ass.
Uncle Warren says, *Uh-huh: You think you smart.*
Well, don't hee-haw to me about how faith
helped you survive the deluge. Save your breath.
Show me. Faith without works ain't worth a fart.
People is hungry. Act out your faith now
by hitching your thanks for God's love to my plow.

IV. Meditation over the Washtub
Exodus 19:4–6a

Oh, I'm hitching my love for Jesus to my plow;
Aunt Sally hums thanksgiving to her Lord,
pausing occasionally to wipe her brow,
scrubbing wet, soapy darks on the washboard.
The clean whites undulate against a breeze
scented with hyacinth and simmering greens.

So this is freedom: the peace of hours like these,
and wages, now, for every house she cleans.
Her singing starts as silence, then her throat
fills with a bubble of expanding praise.
A deeper silence underlies each note:
a lifting mystery, the sky of grace.
Aunt Sally sings, *Yes, Jesus is my friend.*
Hosannas rise like incense on the wind.

Churchgoing

The Lutherans sit stolidly in rows;
only their children feel the holy ghost
that makes them jerk and bobble and almost
destroys the pious atmosphere for those
whose reverence bows their backs as if in work.
The congregation sits, or stands to sing,
or chants the dusty creeds automaton.
Their voices drone like engines, on and on,
and they remain untouched by everything;
confession, praise, or likewise, giving thanks.
The organ that they saved years to afford
repeats the Sunday rhythms song by song,
slow lips recite the credo, smother yawns,
and ask forgiveness for being so bored.

I, too, am wavering on the edge of sleep,
and ask myself again why I have come
to probe the ruins of this dying cult.
I come bearing the cancer of my doubt
as superstitious suffering women come
to touch the magic hem of a saint's robe.

Yet this has served two centuries of men
as more than superstitious cant; they died
believing simply. Women, satisfied

that this was truth, were racked and burned with them
for empty words we moderns merely chant.

We sing a spiritual as the last song,
and we are moved by a peculiar grace
that settles a new aura on the place.
This simple melody, though sung all wrong,
captures exactly what I think is faith.
Were you there when they crucified my Lord?
That slaves should suffer in his agony!
That Christian, slave-owning hypocrisy
nevertheless was by these slaves ignored
as they pitied the poor body of Christ!
Oh, sometimes it causes me to tremble,
that they believe most, who so much have lost.
To be a Christian one must bear a cross.
I think belief is given to the simple
as recompense for what they do not know.

I sit alone, tormented in my heart
by fighting angels, one group black, one white.
The victory is uncertain, but tonight
I'll lie awake again, and try to start
finding the black way back to what we've lost.

Margo Swiss was born in Peterborough, Ontario in 1946. She is the editor of *Poetry As Liturgy* (St. Thomas Poetry Series, 2007). The newest collection of her own poetry is *The Hatching of the Heart* (Poiema Poetry Series, 2015). She teaches Humanities and Creative Writing at York University in Toronto.

Living Water

(John 4:10)

Light rain—
soft, light rain rains.
Living water reigns.

Water
whether wanted
in storm

or warmed
still we are
watered

drenched
sometimes drowse
as roots

earthbound
feed, so we
night-long long

to rise,
to rain
to fall as

light rain—
soft, light rain rains.
Living water reigns.

Women Tell

Women tell of their babies who died:
ones born black as your boot, grey or blue
ones who lived just a day or two
ones who slept with death in their cribs
ones who were spindly and could never suck
ones who were taken before they wore clothes.

Women tell of the nurseries they made:
linens and lamps, assorted notions of joy,
the patient passing of nine months gone
as on a long trip, heavy with love for the unexpected
to be finally rejected by somebody special
who never arrived, a door slammed in the face,
the place they came to a vacant space,
a house abandoned and all swept clean
with only a single sign on the door,
no body lives here any more.

Jill Peláez Baumgaertner was born in the US Midwest in 1948. Her Cuban family heritage is celebrated in her 2001 collection *Finding Cuba*. She is Professor of English and Dean of Humanities and Theological Studies at Wheaton College, and Poetry Editor *for The Christian Century*. Her most-recent poetry collection is *What Cannot Be Fixed* (2014) from the Poiema Poetry Series.

My God, My God

His ragged cry, threads trailing,
a cry full of nails, rips, tears, tēars,
the cry spilling over the full cup
he has taken. Not like a fountain,

bubbling over, but like a mound
of sand, piled high, giving way,
falling grain on grain burying
the burrowing crab almost impossibly

as he does his dark work.
The cry of God to God, desperate,
the question whose answer
is the silence—of the dirt scattered

on the lowered coffin, of the lull
of sea between waves, of the depth
of roots stretched in dark earth
beneath grass, cracking cement,

twisting under pavement, threading
into culverts. *Every night
has something of Gethsemane*,
the theologian says, a shattered

day left behind, then deep night
and sleep and only much later

the awakening to breath
and new light. But for now this

is the present through which
the future becomes the past.
We cling to his cry, our God,
who now knows what we know—

a mute paralysis. No words.
No response. God lives his silence,
our God who now feels his grief,
his questions, his absence.

Grace

Is it the transparency
and lift of air?
Is it release
as when the pebble
flings out of the slingshot
or the tethered dog
suddenly is without lead?

Or is it more like standing
on a dark beach
at midnight,
the surf loud
with its own revolution,
the horizon invisible,
the entire world the threat
of rushing water?

No one who swims
at night in the ocean
feels weightless
embracing armfuls of water

against the ballast
of the waves' fight.

Swimming:
toward the shore lights
or out into the vast bed
of the sea's white fires?

Poem for November

Many trees are mere stencils now,
but some still dazzle, those with light
in their yellow leaves, this even
as November skies stretch mute
and somber.

It is easy this time of year
to dwell on losses and the world
so shattered, even watching this translucent
yellow tree, whose light one could read by,
this blaze against the dimming season.

And we are gathered, each one of us,
in this autumn dilemma,
both anchored and adrift.

Like Eve reaching for Adam's hand
as they stand, stunned,
outside the gates.

Or that child, Mary, who in the silence
after Gabriel's startling news,
wonders, "Should I say yes?"

Or Paul, the persecutor, eyes scaled,
his mouth a thin, straight
line, his heart in its first
ever motion of turning over.

Or two thousand years later
those rabbis at Auschwitz
who put God on trial,
convicted him,
then turned to evening prayer.

Or the aging professor
who said that when he cannot
forgive, he simply acts as if he had.

These images may seem splinters,
fragments scattered and aimless.
But we are not so twisted
that we cannot see the cross's
change from torture into bliss,
from blood and slivers
into the gleam of polished
planks for Christ, arms
raised in victory.

So here we gather
in all of our imperfections,
waiting for song to blaze into the dark
corners, as this year races
toward both finalés and preludes.

Listen. Soon one clear voice will blend
with another. Anchored by the rush
of melody we will catch hold
of the whole breath and timbre
of the moment and together
in this world so prone to drift,
we will see by the cross,
the tree of light, pure music.

Marjorie Stelmach was born in 1948. Among her many awards is the 1994 Marianne Moore Prize for her first book, *Night Drawings*. She has served as visiting poet at the University of Missouri, St. Louis, and has now authored five poetry collections—the newest being *Falter* (Poiema Poetry Series, 2016).

Cellar Door

Years ago somebody decided—I don't know how this conclusion was reached—that the most beautiful phrase in the English language was cellar door.

Don DeLillo, Paris Review, 1993

i. cellar door /cellar door

          Two solid wooden doors hinged to open out
leaning on a sloping ledge against the house. Within,
a wooden stairway leading down into a space
unaccustomed to the sun.

          Entering there on the heels of an adult,
I watched an underworld emerge, lit by the gleam
of Mason jars, shelf on shelf, brass lids glowing
like halos casting light on shapes I only
slowly identified: *apple butter,*
pickled beets, preserves.

          Even in deepest summer, I felt a chill,
breathing packed earth, softening wood. Solemnity
attended every entry, like the shiver and hush
I feel now on the threshold of a church
whose faith is unlike my own, a faith
that seems, nonetheless,
to have expected me.

For years, the doors remained too heavy.
Then one day I found I could, with all my strength,
angle one open, wedge a shoulder into its gap,
and worm myself inside—a feat to mark
a passage—until the door slammed
at my back and the world
went dark.

      For decades, this scene returned in dreams
Except, in dreams, no one missed me, no one came
to search for me. Presumably, someone
came that day. Presumably,
I was saved.

      Or maybe this never happened. Maybe
this is a memory lifted from the etched frontispiece
of a children's book, a story I wedged myself into
thinking there I'd be safe from the slamming
doors of nightmares not my own.
I had my own.

ii. *a sacrament / a sacrilege*

      Walking the blacktop that runs behind the barn
past a gated graveyard, over a rail line and into the hills, I find
I'm numbering the dead: my own; the ones whose stones
are sinking in the churchyard; the road-kill corpses
along the shoulder, their blood deepening
to a shade indistinguishable
by noon from the road's
usual oils.

      Today's fresh kill is a vole. Splayed at my feet,
it spills a scarlet stream from its mouth past pointed teeth
and on to where, in the matted fur, the milk-white
organs glisten. Only the elegant feet remain
unstained. I try to read it as a portent,

but I read it poorly.

My childhood God came down from the pastor's
hand in a disk, parchment-thin, embossed with interwoven signs.
I held him on my tongue, pressed him tight to my palate
where a wash of waters softened the edges of his
perfect tissues—Christ in me, dissolving:
wafer, saliva, watered wine. My flesh
and his, indistinguishable—
the body's darkness
and the world's.

iii. a lavishing / a squandering

It wasn't long before his death, the woman
knelt to bathe his feet, toweling them dry with thick
sheets of hair, pouring over them costly scents:

emoluments suited to anoint the dead? or
oils that, if sold, would have eased
the hardships of the poor?

Even then, I could have argued
either side. Even then, I knew the dead, too,
would always be with us.

iv. a divination / a desecration

Looking again for omens, I open at random
a book of poems and read one line: *I came upon the torso*
of a soul, words that conjure a standard cartoon ghost—
this morning's vole, its pale shape rising from
a broken corpse, playing a cartoon harp,
feet dangling, claws opalescent,
with a tiny halo circling
its resurrected
skull.

Startled, I look back at the page:
I came upon the torso of a seal,
the poem begins.

v. cellar door / sepulcher

It's written, when they lowered him from the cross,
not a bone was broken. It was women who knelt to bathe
the corpse: wounded feet, pierced chest, wrists
opened into gashes from the terrible
weight of human flesh
on nails.

I was taught to kneel at the rail. To take and eat.
This is the torso of a soul born in the year zero to a task
whose weight even God's anointed son
would need thirty years
to learn to bear.

Maybe this never happened / presumably,
I am saved. Even now, I could argue either way.
This is, nonetheless, my story still,
the words of it still beautiful:
cellar door / cellar door
the body's darkness
and the world's.

Robert Cording was born in 1949 in New Jersey. He is the author of eight poetry books including *A Word In My Mouth* (Poiema Poetry Series, 2013), a collection of his Spiritual poems from across his career. He Professor Emeritas and former Barrett Professor of Creative Writing at College of the Holy Cross in Massachusetts.

Rock of Ages

My grandmother, just back from the hospital,
her heart lost and returned for a fourth time,
sings "Rock of Ages," her voice quavering,
graceless, yet determined still to bring
her great-grandson, cranky and tired, to his rest.
His unaged face lies against her
as mine must have when I listened to
the same words floating in air, calling on Christ
to help us in our helplessness. In her voice
I hear her first husband—drunk, raging—
whom she loved and prayed would die.
I hear my grandfather, her second husband,
who provided until he took cancer home
from his job, his lungs a wound that wouldn't heal.
I hear the ghost who wants to lie down
with her now each time she sleeps. I hear
her heart that should have ended but has not,
that sings as if time can only bring pain
and a way to take it away. Outside
the afternoon is locked in gray,
little difference between what lies ahead
and what's already past. Mourning doves
make their sounds of love or sadness.
Of both or neither. I think of the times
when, trembling, I have sung this hymn
in which Christ's wound is a place to hide,
where rabbits and moles, hedgehogs
and bears sleep peacefully in a view of earth
we otherwise never get to see.

Gratitude

In his prison letters, Bonhoeffer is thankful
for a hairbrush, for a pipe and tobacco,
for cigarettes and Schelling's *Morals* Vol. II.
Thankful for stain remover, laxatives,
collar studs, bottled fruit and cooling salts.
For his Bible and hymns praising what is
fearful, which he sings, pacing in circles
for exercise, to his cell walls where he's hung
a reproduction of Durer's *Apocalypse*.
He's thankful for letters from his parents
and friends that lead him back home,
and for the pain of memory's arrival,
his orderly room of books and prints too far
from the nightly sobs of a prisoner
in the next cell whom Bonhoeffer does not know
how to comfort, though he believes religion
begins with a neighbor who is within reach.
He's thankful for the few hours outside
in the prison yard, and for the half-strangled
laughter between inmates as they sit together
under a chestnut tree. He's thankful even
for a small ant hill, and for the ants that are
all purpose and clear decision. For the two
lime trees that mumble audibly with the workings
of bees in June and especially for the warm
laying on of sun that tells him he's a man
created of earth and not of air and thoughts.
He's thankful for minutes when his reading
and writing fill up the emptiness of time,
and for those moments when he sees himself
as a small figure in a vast, unrolling scroll,
though mostly he looks out over the plains
of ignorance inside himself. And for that,
too, he's thankful: for the self who asks,
Who am I?—the man who steps cheerfully

from this cell and speaks easily to his jailers,
or the man who is restless and trembling
with anger and despair as cities burn and Jews
are herded into railroad cars—can
without an answer, say finally, *I am thine,*
to a God who lives each day,
as Bonhoeffer must, in the knowledge
of what has been done, is still being done,
his gift a refusal to leave his suffering, for which,
even as the rope is placed around his neck
and pulled tight, Bonhoeffer is utterly grateful.

Reading George Herbert

All he ever wanted was to disappear.
But he kept coming upon himself
as if he were a character in a story
who, despite his best efforts to understand,
remained inscrutable. He tried
to keep straight the difference between
who the author said he was and who he
thought he was. He told himself again
and again that God was closer to him
than he was to himself. Still, he couldn't

close the distance. He was always getting
lost in his own plot, going off in all
the wrong directions. His own words
never helped, being always full of
a wild hunger, self-propulsive.
Prayer helped. But even when he heard
a melody not his own, when he'd try
to sing it, what came out of him
was off-key and horribly out of tune.

Each day he went to war against himself,
but he could never disarm himself.
Yet, waking, he'd often relish the new day,
tasting the sweetness of the world
he accepted as an undeserved gift.
And, in its clear and shimmering air,
he'd sometimes see a road that ran straight
to the open door of paradise,
though the moment he started walking,

the day would be diminished by the weight
of clouds that gradually lugged themselves
all the way to the horizon. How could he
not help but think, *sure, of course,*
just as I expected, just what I deserved?
Once, having traveled farther
from himself than he'd ever been,
he believed he heard God saying, *Yes, this way*
come ahead, enter, but he was only human,
and thought the voice must be his own.

In Between

They had reasons to believe in God.
Miracles helped. And their after-effects
must have lingered for a time, but then,
the disciples needed to start walking again,
one town to another, nothing in between
but the hot, dusty road and a desert
of sand and rock where not one thing
required a moment's appreciation.
Just one sandaled foot in front of another
and way too much time to consider
the whole bed-through-the-roof episode
or the uncrossable valley between sleeping
and death. *What did we really see?*

the disciples must have asked themselves
as they walked with their Teacher,
who always seemed near and far at once.

And what were they to make of that question
he would not stop asking, and asked,
they suspected, as if he were mocking them—
Who do you say I am, who do you say I am?
They probably wished they had more time
to think about how to answer and yet
they knew, too, that time was exactly
what they had. They must have wondered,
Is he asking, who he is or who we say he is?
And, *What does it matter who we say he is?*
Every day brought different questions—
Do we need to know who we are, to answer?
Is who we are, the same as who we are
in relation to him? And different answers.

Some days their Teacher seemed a story
that was living and some days a story
they were not sure how they would ever tell.
It could not have been easy to believe
they would be saved by someone
who told them he was headed straight
for a cross. And then it happened.
And they felt like witnesses to an event
they had never wanted, and one
that had arrived without their being
ready for it. They must have known
afterward that theirs would be
a ridiculous and mulish faith
taking place in between the arousals
of good bread and wine, and a God
who was felt most now that he was gone.

Dana Gioia was born in 1950 in California. He has five poetry collections, including *Interrogations at Noon*—which won the 2002 American Book Award—and his latest, *99 Poems: New & Selected* (Graywolf, 2016). He was the chair for the National Endowment for the Arts between 2003 and 2009. Gioia teaches at the University of Southern California.

For The Birth of Christ

Now is the season of our long regret
When all the borrowed levities conspire
To hide the hopeless balance of our debt.

The winter air grows sharp with our desire,
And all the ancient hungers reappear.
We come to watch for you, a child of fire.

Again the shining city seems so near.
Send down the flaming stairs into the night
Before our dreams have vanished with the year.

If lesser visions charmed a summer's night,
We knew they lacked the necessary pain.
You bring no season of rehearsed delight.

And requiems combine with our refrain.
For with your birth a part of us will die.
Alone, we cry the coming of your reign.

Will you, o fiery child, make no reply?

Prayer

Echo of the clocktower, footstep
in the alleyway, sweep
of the wind sifting the leaves.

Jeweller of the spiderweb, connoisseur
of autumn's opulence, blade of lightning
harvesting the sky.

Keeper of the small gate, choreographer
of entrances and exits, midnight
whisper travelling the wires.

Seducer, healer, deity or thief,
I will see you soon enough—
in the shadow of the rainfall,

in the brief violet darkening a sunset—
but until then I pray watch over him
as a mountain guards its covert ore

and the harsh falcon its flightless young.

Pentecost

After the death of our son

Neither the sorrows of afternoon, waiting in the silent house,
Nor the night no sleep relieves, when memory
Repeats its prosecution.

Nor the morning's ache for dream's illusion, nor any prayers
Improvised to an unknowable god
Can extinguish the flame.

We are not as we were. Death has been our pentecost,
And our innocence consumed by these implacable
Tongues of fire.

Comfort me with stones. Quench my thirst with sand.
I offer you this scarred and guilty hand
Until others mix our ashes.

The Archbishop

for a famous critic

O, do not disturb the Archbishop,
Asleep in his ivory chair.
You must send all the workers away,
Though the church is in need of repair.

His Reverence is tired from preaching
To the halt, and the lame, and the blind.
Their spiritual needs are unsubtle,
Their notions of God unrefined.

The Lord washed the feet of His servants.
"The first shall be last," He advised.
The Archbishop's edition of Matthew
Has that troublesome passage revised.

The Archbishop declines to wear glasses,
So his sense of the world grows dim.
He thinks that the crowds at Masses
Have gathered in honor of him.

In the crypt of the limestone cathedral
A friar recopies St. Mark,
A num serves stew to a novice,
A choirboy sobs in the dark.

While high in the chancery office
His Reverence studies the glass,
Wondering which of his vestments
Would look best at Palm Sunday Mass.

The saints in their weather-stained niches
Weep as the Vespers are read,
And the beggars sleep on the church steps,
And the orphans retire unfed.

On Easter the Lord is arisen
While the Archbishop breakfasts in bed,
And the humble shall find resurrection,
And the dead shall lie down with the dead.

Prayer at Winter Solstice

Blessed is the road that keeps us homeless.
Blessed is the mountain that blocks our way.

Blessed are hunger and thirst, loneliness and all forms of desire.
Blessed is the labor that exhausts us without end.

Blessed are the night and the darkness that blinds us.
Blessed is the cold that teaches us to feel.

Blessed are the cat, the child, the cricket, and the crow.
Blessed is the hawk devouring the hare.

Blessed are the saint and the sinner who redeem each other.
Blessed are the dead calm in their perfection.

Blessed is the pain that humbles us.
Blessed is the distance that bars our joy.

Blessed is this shortest day that makes us long for light.
Blessed is the love that in losing we discover.

Homage to Søren Kierkegaard

> *"Work out your own salvation*
> *with fear and trembling."*

I was already an old man when I was born.
Small with a curved back, he dragged his leg when walking
the streets of Copenhagen. "Little Kierkegaard,"
they called him. Some meant it kindly. *The more one suffers*
the more one acquires a sense of the comic.
His hair rose in waves six inches above his head.
Save me, O God, from ever becoming sure.

What good is faith if it is not irrational?

Christianity requires a conviction of sin.
As a boy tending sheep on the frozen heath,
his starving father cursed God for his cruelty.
His fortunes changed. He grew rich and married well.
His father knew these blessings were God's punishment.
All would be stripped away. His beautiful wife died,
then five of his children. Crippled Soren survived.
The self-consuming sickness unto death is despair.

What the age needs is not a genius but a martyr.
Soren fell in love, proposed, then broke the engagement.
No one, he thought, could bear his presence daily.
My sorrow is my castle. His books were read
but ridiculed. Cartoons mocked his deformities.
His private journals fill seven thousand pages.
You could read them all, he claimed, and still not know him.
He who explains this riddle explains my life.

*When everyone is Christian, Christianity
does not exist. The crowd is untruth.* Remember
we stand alone before God in fear and trembling.
At forty-two he collapsed on his daily walk.
Dying he seemed radiant. His skin had become
almost transparent. He refused communion
from the established church. His grave has no headstone.
Now with God's help I shall at last become myself.

Laurie Klein was born in Wisconsin in 1950, and now lives in Washington State. Her honors include the 2007 Thomas Merton Poetry of the Sacred Award, and she is one of the founding editors of *Rock & Sling*. Her first full-length poetry collection is *Where The Sky Opens* (Poiema Poetry Series, 2015).

Washed Up

Some tunes move the foot, inside a shoe,
some elevate the soul, while others,
numinous as the song of Zion, play on
without us.
            Remember winging it?
Fingers and toes and spirits
surrendered to more than the moment,
hearts drafting off each other,
                    daring
as swifts, weaving aerial fractals, our voices
ascending a groove, a line of thought,
into the upper reaches, then coasting
into rarified silence—the Mystery
humming within and
               beyond all things.
No one leads the singing as you did, love.
No one else intuits my pulse
and impulse, improvising
new settings befitting
             the inner lark.
Old friends ask about you, tender
their prayers. I am counting on this:
how greatly you're loved,
and the kingdom emerging
in guises we never knew.

Unbelief

Begin with the body:
holy, breathing, real—how we *know*;
later, call it a book of curves,
home, riddled with contradictions.

Ask those who design, and
by design, deceive: "Which is truer?
a coin toss, or vote?
an aqueduct, or a well of salvation?
a seven-veil dance worth one life,
or half a kingdom?"

Or picture
Moses and Paul, head-to-head,
curled around time, two halves,
one voice, their ropey, blue-collar
topography riveting as a river
flicking a skipped stone,
as if each word cast is a net
enclosing a silver fish—arc
against air—half a second
and one small glimmer
all it takes to re-aim a skeptic's gaze.

The Back Forty

Bean thinks about things, while walking—
like the number forty:

Pat Tillman's retired red jersey
or winks in a power nap,
the Bible's wilderness days of temptation,
direct dial code for Romania,
full-time work, the days of Lent,

not to mention the negative point
where Fahrenheit matches Celsius,

or Venus in retrograde,
and the Nebra Sky Disk—forty perforations
rimming a Bronze Age timepiece, as if
the ancients wearied of notching sticks
to reckon the wonder of each solar year,

and the fetus, turning, in watery silence,

Noah, bending before the rain,
and later, one green sprig in a beak—

or, egg to old age, the life spans
of Monarchs, drones, those fruit flies
barnstorming the bowl of peaches,

and what about forty years
of sandals slapping the Sinai sands,
and skybread, and walking out Torah,

or the average life of the lumbering hippo
and Asian elephant, the lion
and bare-eyed cockatoo?—

and now, forty years together:
wild, savory, perilous, graced.

Rowan Williams was born in Swansea, Wales in 1950. His many books include the compilation: *The Poems of Rowan Williams* (Carcanet, 2014). He served as the Archbishop of Canterbury from 2002 to 2012. In 2013 he was given a seat in the House of Lords and the title Lord Williams of Oystermouth. He is also Master of Magdalene College in Cambridge.

Advent Calendar

He will come like last leaf's fall.
One night when the November wind
has flayed the trees to bone, and earth
wakes choking on the mould,
the soft shroud's folding.

He will come like frost.
One morning when the shrinking earth
opens on mist, to find itself
arrested in the net
of alien, sword-set beauty.

He will come like dark.
One evening when the bursting red
December sun draws up the sheet
and penny-masks its eye to yield
the star-snowed fields of sky.

He will come, will come,
will come like crying in the night,
like blood, like breaking,
as the earth writhes to toss him free.
He will come like child.

Resurrection: Borgo San Sepolcro

Today it is time. Warm enough, finally,
to ease the lids apart, the wax lips of a breaking bud
defeated by the steady push, hour after hour,
opening to show wet and dark, a tongue exploring,
an eye shrinking against the dawn. Light
like a fishing line draws its catch straight up,
then slackens for a second. The flat foot drops,
the shoulders sag. Here is the world again, well-known,
the dawn greeted in snoring dreams of a familiar
winter everyone prefers. So the black eyes
fixed half-open, start to search, ravenous,
imperative, they look for pits, for hollows where
their flood can be decanted, look
for rooms ready for commandeering, ready
to be defeated by the push, the green implacable
rising. So he pauses, gathering the strength
in his flat foot, as the perspective buckles under him,
and the dreamers lean dangerously inwards. Contained,
exhausted, hungry, death running off his limbs like
drops
from a shower, gathering himself. We wait,
paralysed as if in dreams, for his spring.

Nagasaki: Midori's Rosary

The air is full of blurred words. Something
has changed in the war's weather. The children
(whose children will show me this) have been sent
to the country. In the radiology lab,
Takashi fiddles, listening to the ticking bomb
in his blood cells, thinks, once, piercingly,
of her hands and small mouth, knotting him in
to the long recital of silent lives

under the city's surface, the ripple of blurred Latin,
changing nothing in the weather of death and confession,
thinks once, in mid-morning, of a kitchen floor, flash-frozen.

When, in the starburst's centre,
the little black mouth opens, then clenches,
and the flaying wind smoothes down the grass
and prints its news black on bright blinding
walls, when it sucks back the milk
and breath and skin, and all the world's vowels
drown in flayed throats, the hard things,
bone and tooth, fuse into consonants of stone,
Midori's beads melt in a single mass
around the shadow with its blackened hands
carved with their little weeping lips.

Days earlier, in Hiroshima, in what was left
of the clinic chapel, little Don Pedro, turning
from the altar to say, The Lord be with you,
heard, suddenly, what he was about to claim,
seeing the black lips, the melted bones,
and so, he said, he stood, his small mouth
open, he never knew how long, his hands
out like a starburst, while the dialogue
of stony voiceless consonants ground across
the floor, like gravel in the wind, and the two
black mouths opened against each other,

Nobody knowing for a while
which one would swallow which.

Brad Davis was born in San Diego in 1952. He served on the faculty of Pomfret School in Connecticut for 29 years, and has taught at College of the Holy Cross and at Eastern Connecticut State University. His poetry books include *Opening King David* (2011) and *Still Working It Out* (Poiema Poetry Series, 2014).

After A Snowfall

Above a shapeless field, the fine up-swept tip of a redtail's wing.
On an unplowed road, euphoria at spotting it suddenly.
Then later over tea, delight in recalling the moment's perfection.
And now this.
                    If all were mere necessity, then why such beauty?
We are perhaps the only witness to what we think we see
and long to enter—a sacred grove, a new earth, a father's well-
prepared welcome home—and so leave behind all want, all sorrow
for what never fails to spoil our truest effort.
                                    My wish:
to hold close the wide, miraculous world I lumber through
shouting, *There!* and *Over Here!* or waving subtly whenever
words or sudden motion might send it fleeing—everywhere rejoicing.

What I Answered

for DLD

It was, of course, the cancer that killed her.
She and I were alone in the hospital room.
You were at the nurses' station, I think,
or in the bathroom, or picking up lunch.
The sun was bright through the window.
We were holding hands and I had just said
something about God. Or faith. Or maybe
about Schuller, or catching the closing night
of a Graham crusade on the tube. In any case,

I had spoken from my love for her, and you know
how I loved her, how easily we laughed together.
Her next words to me were clear and soft.
The tone of her voice, natural. Even calm.
I believe she wanted to know: *Am I dying?*
Yes. It never occurred to me to say anything else.
Besides, she always could see through a lie.
She looked over at me, then away at the window.
Slowly she closed her eyes, squeezed my hand.

No one had prepared me for that silence.
I'll never forget the time she told me how
she enjoyed bragging to her customers
at the laundromat about her daughter being
married to a priest, and how it never failed to raise
their thick, French Catholic eyebrows. I don't
remember wearing my collar to the hospital that day.
Or why I have taken so long to tell you this.
She and I sat there in the bright room holding hands.

Still Working It Out

*for Robin Needham, killed
in the 2004 Christmas tsunami*

Something
shuddered in the unfathomable

dark, and a wave
shouldered forth

like an eighteen wheeler
skidding sideways

into oncoming traffic—a wave

inhering by the power

of a word lovely
as snow on a navy sleeve,

the same word
that shuddered in each

dark cell of the dead
Christ, a wave shouldering forth

like a new heaven, new
earth, clearing away

the old, the impossible—a wave,
a word, terrible as it is

great, great as it is holy
and terrible.

Vocation

The world is a bright field
and I a laborer

enlisted by a brighter love, a light
delighted to illumine

every curve and canyon,
ice cap and prairie,

the scuffed floor tiles in this
small town cafe, each

face at work or tarrying
here. Like Simone, barista

whom my wife wants our friend
Geoff to meet; or Ian

from Ireland who speaks well
of his Savior to anyone

with time and ears to hear; or kind
Christine who runs the place;

or Ahmed and his chatty band
of schoolmate brothers

whose prophet has no peer.
This is the bright

world, my field, little universe
that I will fail—if I fail

to attend to each part and the whole
and the light that delights

to illumine shop, river, hedgerow,
village and villager.

Mark Jarman was born in Kentucky in 1952. His poetry demonstrates his dedication to traditional poetic forms, as does the anthology, *Rebel Angels: 25 Poets of the New Formalism* (1996), which he co-edited. He is Professor of English at Vanderbilt University, in Nashville. His *Bone Fires: New and Selected Poems* (Sarabande, 2011) received the Balcones Poetry Prize.

Unholy Sonnet #22

What will we give up in the after life,
When we have been enhanced to a higher power
And all the goodness of the body made so pure
It's quantum leap will have to feel like loss?
In our spirit flesh, *pneumatikon*
(Though the Greek sounds like a mattress): to see
Will be to take; to wish for, have; to sigh
Will be the sign of utter satisfaction.
But what about that instant of desire
Before we're granted, the rapturous waiting
On this side of epiphany and climax?
Without the lapse of time, we'll lose that pleasure,
The unique arousal of previsioning,
The thrill in scenting that first cup of coffee.

Unholy Sonnet #28

I'll bet the final reckoning's like this:
That brilliant day in Swansea, in the park
Across the street from Thomas's birthplace,
My camera pointed everywhere to mark
In light the record of our happiness,
My daughters on the swings, his poetry
Among the garden stones, the Bristol Channel—
The North Atlantic's Welsh and English kennel—

Beyond the Mumbles Lighthouse. You could see
All the way to heaven's old address.
I thought I caught is all, a floating spark
Of memory that film would surely fix,
Only to learn the cog-slipped roll was dark
And blank as Lethe and the River Styx.

Prayer for Our Daughters

May they never be lonely at parties
Or wait for mail from people they haven't written
Or still in middle age ask God for favors
Or forbid their children things they were never forbidden.

May hatred be like a habit they never developed
And can't see the point of, like gambling or heavy drinking.
If they forget themselves, may it be in music
Or the kind of prayer that makes a garden of thinking.

May they enter the coming century
Like swans under a bridge into enchantment
And take with them enough of this century
To assure their grandchildren it really happened.

May they find a place to love, without nostalgia
For some place else that they can never go back to.
And may they find themselves, as we have found them,
Complete at each stage of their lives, each part they add to.

May they be themselves, long after we've stopped watching.
May they return from every kind of suffering
(Except the last, which doesn't bear repeating)
And be themselves again, both blessed and blessing.

At the Communion Rail

When, about to receive the Host for the first time,
I cup my hands as I was never taught
and listen to the priest describe the meaning
of the translucent disc of holy starch,
as I am lifting it, pinched, towards my mouth,
ready too for the goblet of red liquor—
a spirit speaks inside me, fiercer, stricter
than an angry parent's rote, an old man's voice,
outraged but with the weakness of the deathbed,
gasping and rasping in a chamber of my heart,
"What do you think you are doing? What *are* you doing?"
And into that same chamber, I shout back—
only I can hear this—I shout back
a response never considered for this rite:
"I'm doing this! To hell with you! I'm doing it!"

After the Scourging

He crawls like a man toward water in the desert,
back to the mocking robe, dropped at the feet
of two attendant, worried-looking angels
who are under orders not to intervene.

Will he become more godlike in the robe
or less a disfigured god and more a man?

"If I can only get this put back on . . ."
could be the meaning in his blackened eyes,
the determination bleeding from his fingers
as they claw the rumpled cloth into his grip:
"If I can put this on, I will stand up."

After Murillo

John Terpstra was born in Ontario in 1953. He is a carpenter and cabinet-maker, as well as a poet and nonfiction writer. His fourth nonfiction book is *The House with the Parapet Wall* (2014) and his numerous poetry collections include *Disarmament* (2003) and *Brilliant Falls* (2013): these titles are from Gaspereau Press. He and his wife live in downtown Hamilton.

Near–Annunciation at Carroll's Point

First try, the bird dropped
                              from the sky,
belly-flopping the surface
that separates our two worlds,
and came up empty.
                              He rose again
and wung away
in easy, languorous strokes,
as if it was all part of the plan.

Hunger returned him.
But whose?

What surprises us now, despite
our dragnet of the seven seas,

is that our lady
was not
              a first or only choice.

I am but a carpenter
sitting on a bench, beside water
yet have observed
more than one
              slim silver beauty

who had but a single
                    premonitory moment

to ponder who or what
                    that brilliance meant
                    which filled the sky
before being plucked from their lives.

The dying-to-self
                    our mothers did so well
a little something
they picked up on the fly.

New Year, Good Work

The tools of the trade lay scattered on the floor
below the altar, migrating to its surface
(protected under plywood and a cloth tarp),
only after the first few days, when the fine mist
of wood dust that settled over the pews and furnishings
helped us to feel more at ease in this space
now sanctified to our labour.
Church interior as work-site.
I can think of worse ways to begin the year.

Moving through the motions of ritual
attendance to table saw, mitre saw,
in mindful repetition, alert, thinking
only of the blade, the cut, its closeness
to the mark, each length and angle made
to match another, to join in such perfection
as can be achieved on this job, in this lifetime.
And it's always fresh cut to fresh cut,
and there's something to that, but I can't think what.

A question formed itself as we chewed cuds
at break time, prompted by the vaulted ceiling
and the heartfelt, volunteer labour
of the two who started this project, who made

not a complete botch, but thank God
had no chainsaw handy to trim the wainscot.
The question? Ah, yes: our patron in this place,
was he a finish carpenter, or rough?

A lot of fancy woodwork's been performed
on his behalf. The romantic version has him
leaned over a plank, his two hands gripped
on a bench plane, a long shaving furled
round his wrist: the scroll that we apprentice-priests
of woodcraft must uncurl, to read the grain
wherein lies hid the meaning of life and death
and pretty much everything in between.

Did he enjoy the fine work, or prefer
to hammer studs; to kiss that sixteenth of an inch,
or was close enough, good enough?
What were his tolerances, professionally?
Could he make it less than perfect? Did he measure
once? And how did he balance the desire to do it well
with the need to get it done?

These and other questions will be answered
Sunday morning by his current rep,
who'll stand behind the pulpit we've restored,
and packed our tools, and collected and swept
the scraps and shavings, and vacuumed up the dust—
though later we will hear that the incense of our craft
and labour lingered in the sanctuary air that day,
as answered prayer for good work, done—
which is all we need to know, and answer enough.

Scott Cairns was born in Tacoma, Washington, in 1954. He is the author of eight poetry books, including *Slow Pilgrim: The Collected Poems* (Paraclete Press, 2015). He is Professor of English at the University of Missouri, and is the recipient of the 2014 Denise Levertov Award.

Possible Answers to Prayer

Your petitions—though they continue to bear
just the one signature—have been duly recorded.
Your anxieties—despite their constant,

relatively narrow scope and inadvertent
entertainment value—nonetheless serve
to bring your person vividly to mind.

Your repentance—all but obscured beneath
a burgeoning, yellow fog of frankly more
conspicuous resentment—is sufficient.

Your intermittent concern for the sick,
the suffering, the needy poor is sometimes
recognizable to me, if not to them.

Your angers, your zeal, your lipsmackingly
righteous indignation toward the many
whose habits and sympathies offend you—

these must burn away before you'll apprehend
how near I am, with what fervor I adore
precisely these, the several who rouse your passions.

Jonah's Imprisonment

What might one then expect when fleeing the Lord's imperative? Well, an obstacle of one or another sort—uneasiness of mind, missed connections, ungenerous companions, perhaps an enormous fish.

That Jonah was without joy at the prospect of Nineveh is well recorded. Less famous is his disinclination for any intercourse with unbelievers, whom he, out of habit, identified as the unwashed. From birth, he had been protected from most embarrassments: body odor, poorly cooked food, substandard grammar. And so the Lord, in His compassion, undertook to deliver Jonah from his own sin—not fastidiousness as such, only Jonah's insistence upon it.

His time in the fish's belly was like death. At the very least it smelled like death to Jonah. In retrospect, the experience, fully imagined, might still provoke a necessary sense of how the body, unadorned by ointments, oils, or silk is little more than meat, mere meat for fishes. And if, in that confusion of digesting debris, Jonah chose to distinguish himself from other meat, he would have to come up with other criteria, and pretty soon.

Consider any brute swimmer driving with all his energies against the tide; notice how ineffectual (and potentially comic) the effort appears from the chalk white cliffs above.

Gross facts aside, the monster was Jonah's deliverance, a more than sufficient transportation to a more likely perspective, from which Jonah was then fully willing to embrace anybody.

Parable

To what might this slow puzzle be
       compared? The rabbi is perplexed.

That said, please bear in mind the rabbi
        has a taste for fraught perplexities.

Comparisons have long obtained
        for those enamored of the word

a measure of requital, have
        tendered—just here, for instance—a

momentary take, a likely
        likening, not to be unduly

honored as anything, well,
        conclusive, but categorically

toward. Still, I love these textures
        on the tongue, and love the way

their taste and feel so often serve
        to spin the body and the mind

into one vertiginous
        assemblage. And so, one asks, to what

slight figure might The Vast and
        Inexplicable compare? A mist

that penetrates the bone? The looming
        sea? The all but endless and

unyielding green expanse above?
        Or, say, the laden word whose compass

and whose burdens turn a multitude
        of keen articulations, full

none of which quite seems to satisfy.

Idiot Psalm 1

—a psalm of Isaak, accompanied by Jew's harp.

O God Belovéd if obliquely so,
    dimly apprehended in the midst
    of this, the fraught obscuring fog
    of my insufficiently capacious ken,
    Ostensible Lover of our kind—while
    apparently aloof—allow
    that I might glimpse once more
    Your shadow in the land, avail
    for me, a second time, the sense
    of dire Presence in the pulsing
    hollow near the heart.
Once more, O Lord, from Your Enormity incline
    your Face to shine upon Your servant, shy
    of immolation, if You will.

Idiot Psalm 5

—a psalm of Isaak raised in unaccustomed stillness

With unclean lips, at least, and yea
    with unclean hands, encumbered heart,
    congested, lo these many years,
    with no small measure of regret,
    and sin's particulate debris,
with these and countless other dear
    impediments, I stoop to find
    my knees. And on occasion You,
    Whose dimly figured Face I dare
    pursue to searing clarity,
    have condescended, acquiesced
    to grant what little I might bear.

Idiot Psalm 6

—a psalm of Isaak, hoarsely sung.

And yet again the wicked in his arrogance,
    in his acutely hemmed and tapered sense
    of self has found
    sufficient opportunity to hound
    the lowly.
And yet again, Great Enabler, the lowly,
    draped in their accustomed modesty
    and threadbare suits bereft
    have seized the chance to suffer quietly, stage left.
Therefore, now again, I puzzle why,
    O Holy Silence, why
    do You appear to bide unheeding
    some great distance hence?
Why, O Blithely *Un*apparent, do you remain
    serenely imperceptible, even to our thinning
    crew who stand here blinking at the sky?
I have no stomach for the newspapers, no heart
    for the brilliant, flat-screen lit catalog
    of woes, though every item flickers,
    one admits, wondrously produced
    and duly sponsored.
See here. The wicked boasts about his late
    successes, the grasping man complains
    that he is cheated of his share, while all
    the while the self-concerned continue
    banking largely on Your accustomed reticence,
    and must needs let out their trousers still
    several measures more, having wagered well.
Pinched beneath their spinning machinations
    and all their neat machines,
    we grind our teeth,
    yea, even as we sleep.

Andrew Lansdown was born in Western Australia in 1954. He has published five books of fiction, and more than ten collections of poetry, including *Far From Home: Poems of Faith, Grief and Gladness* (2010). He has twice won the Western Australian Premier's Prize for poetry. He and his family live in Perth.

The Colour of Life

Why is it that here in this cafe,
a hard wind harmless on the window,
a bright fire coughing in the grate,
scones and tea on the table, I feel

suddenly, strangely sad? Why is it,
and what? A loneliness, a longing—
not, it seems, in spite of, but
because of, the loveliest of things.

It is the colour of life. *Sabi*
the haiku poets would say. I say
too much. I break a scone and steam
wafts from the wound, like

the spirit of a just man, going home.

Prayer

Oh, for my mother in her pain,
Almighty and all-loving Lord,
I come to plead with you again.

For years her body's been a bane
That's put all gladness to the sword:
Oh, for my mother in her pain!

Too much misery makes a stain
To black all light and block all laud:
I come to plead with you again.

Today at least relieve the strain
And give reprieve as a reward,
Oh, for my mother in her pain.

I know there is no other Name.
Despite the fact my faith is flawed,
I come to plead with you again.

Although my many sins maintain
That I deserve to be ignored—
Oh, for my mother in her pain
I come to plead with you again!

Kangaroos

Silent as the light-
ly falling rain,
kangaroos are bounding
in a single file
across the near paddock.

A buck, a doe, a joey,
diminishing in size
like a trick
of perspective, going
fast, their tails

working up and down
like the handle of a pump,
spring-loading
their legs for each jump.

Without pause, the buck

leaps the fence
but the smaller two balk
at the last moment.
Now, without momentum,
they are without hope

of hurdling the wire.
They race along the fence,
the curve of their down-
swinging tails touching
the angle of their up-

springing heels. It is
no use. The barrier
is unbroken. Finally
they stop, stand still
and stare into the bush.

Two grey skittle-shapes,
thalidomide paws
clasped to their chests.
Bewildered they gaze back
across the open paddock

to where a rainbow has
raised a bright crosier
to bless the dreadful world.

Black Bamboo

i
Empathy today
with the ebony bamboo—
this empty feeling.

ii
This feeling—something
that's escaped from the centre
of a bamboo cane.

iii
Hollow . . . I suppose
the bamboo by my window
always feels this way.

iv
Again I wake
with a hollow feeling—oh,
my bamboo heart!

v
Hollow, like the black
bamboo . . . if only I had
its composure, too.

vi
Lord, may not music
come from emptiness? Oh make
a flute of my heart!

Nicholas **Samaras** was born in England in 1954, has lived on the Greek isle of Patmos, and now lives in the US. He is the 1991 winner of the Yale Series of Younger Poets Award for his debut collection *Hands of the Saddlemaker*. His recent book—*American Psalm, World Psalm* (Ashland, 2014)—consists of 150 of the poet's own psalms.

The Unpronounceable Psalm

I couldn't wrap my mouth around the vowel of your name.
Your name, a cave of blue wind that burrows and delves
endlessly, that rings off the walls of my drumming, lilting heart,
through the tiny pulsations of my wrists, the blood in my neck.
I couldn't hold the energy of your name in my mouth
that was like trying to utter the crackle of lightning,
as if my teeth would break from its pronunciation.
I am dwarfed in the face of your magnitude,
O you whom I can't articulate. O you of fluency
and eloquence whom I can't fully express, my words
are only the echo of you that rings within my soul, my soul
a cave of blue wind that houses the draft of you,
the eternal vowel of you I can't wrap my mouth around.
Lord, Lord, as close as I may gather, as close as I may say.

Exodus

The Lord was as simple as walking
into evening. We stepped out of our lives.
The tea on the fire, the bread in the bowl.
My book lying face up, open at the page.
Choosing the Lord was as simple as walking
forward, the trust of a child holding onto you,
your own trust settled like believing,
the doors open onto a cool, unleavened evening.

The Psalm of Not

Not breath, but breathing.
Not me, but Christ in me.
Not me, but the Holy Spirit in me.
Not breath, but breathing.
Not justification, but repentance.
Not me, but my neighbor first.
Not time given, but time used.
Not my chance, but my helping
others find their chance.
Not breath, but breathing.
Not a prayer based on need or fear,
but a prayer based on love.
Not the act, but the action.
Not me, but the ancestors comprising me.
Not my hands, but the craft of my hands.
Not me, but my daughter and my son.
Not me, but my father in me, glimmering.
Not breath, but breathing.

Psalm as the Breath of God

Sheen of wind off the bluest harbor.
The lattices of gold-leafed light.
Anything felt deeply is a mystery, or can be.
The way theology only whispers.
The presence of God
is like breath on a windowpane. I think
of alpine wind skittered over snow. God's breath
is poetry. God's breath, the scent of snow drifting
down at midnight. Windowpanes haunted
by the gauze of curtains, the rise and fall of sleeping air.
We who practice the art of writing,
recording our feelings, in effect
put down our breathing upon the page—
breath become devotion.
The slow exhalation that is understanding.
Exhalation that is acceptance.
In this small way, we are able to capture
the breath of God—both movement and stillness.
Lord, with your breathing as my conscience,
every breath I take is one breath
closer to you. The breath that is Samaras
and is the breath of the Lord within me.
Intone a cooling breeze, sing the clarity of the desert.
Murmur the chant of the page. Oh, sing my breathing voice.

Elemental Psalm

I was salt, so the Lord mined me.
I came as a field of silvery trees
laden with olives hardened by frost,
a rough crop with some spots
tender to rottenness, some spots
coarse and unusable, bruised

157

and eaten on the edge.
So, the Lord cut from me the unusable
and, from the rest of me, he made pure oil.
I was coal, so the Lord impressed me.
I was parched, so the Lord planted
deeper within me, until it took
years of digging to break the surface.
I was salt.
The Lord mined.
In the darkness, there is no greater
reprieve than a spark.
In the desert, there is no miracle
greater than cold water.

Vespers

Night is dark ink. No sound
but the muffled movements of the living.

Three polite taps at the grey slats of the guest door.
Beneath it, the bobbing red glow of a kerosene lamp

diminishing. The eleventh hour in Byzantium. Outside,
the faint howl of a wolf beyond the slumbering ravine.

I lumber up. Two shadows converge downstairs in the tiny room.
Haloed, wooden faces peer out from the soft gloom.

A drawn curtain the colour of dried blood. We rustle
the hundred years of brocade with our cracked voices.

You give me the Psalter to begin and stand next to me,
a column of dark light. I stammer over the language,

aching from sleep, aching from yesterday's climb

through the olive ravine, the green mansion, the parched

resting in the hollow of the jungle. With my rooms back home
and bills arriving, with the modern world in decline, who are we

to stand away and sing? Who are we not to?
Black monastic, with your liver disease neither advancing

nor remitting, living on this mountain-side in bliss
without this century's medicine, you harmonise through the hymnody.

We chant to the hours waning, troparia of loss and receipt,
joy and sorrow. I study the bright, blazing faces of paint

and ancient light, my hands trembling to hold the book steady
while I view the black-gold side of your face in the candleglow and
shadow.

Mary Karr was born in Texas in 1955. She is the author of the best-selling memoir *The Liars Club*, which was a *New York Times* bestseller for over a year. She is also the Peck Professor of English at Syracuse University. Her fourth poetry collection *Sinners Welcome* (2006) was published by HarperCollins.

Who the Meek Are Not

Not the bristle-bearded Igors bent
under burlap sacks, not peasants knee-deep
in the rice-paddy muck,
nor the serfs whose quarter-moon sickles
make the wheat fall in waves
they don't get to eat. My friend the Franciscan
nun says we misread
that word *meek* in the Bible verse that blesses them.
To understand the meek
(she says) picture a great stallion at full gallop
in a meadow, who—
at his master's voice—seizes up to a stunned
but instant halt.
So with the strain of holding that great power
in check, the muscles
along the arched neck keep eddying,
and only the velvet ears
prick forward, awaiting the next order.

Disgraceland

Before my first communion at 40, I clung
    to doubt as Satan spider-like stalked
        the orb of dark surrounding Eden
            for a wormhole into paradise.

God had first formed me in the womb
    small as a bite of burger.
        Once my lungs were done
            He sailed a soul like a lit arrow

to inflame me. Maybe that piercing
    made me howl at birth,
        or the masked creatures
            whose scalpel cut a lightning bolt to free me—

I was hoisted by the heels and swatted, fed
    and hauled through rooms. Time-lapse photos show
        my fingers grew past crayon outlines,
            my feet came to fill spike heels.

Eventually, I lurched out to kiss the wrong mouths,
    get stewed, and sulk around. Christ always stood
        to one side with a glass of water.
        I swatted the sap away.

When my thirst got great enough
    to ask, a stream welled up inside;
        some jade wave buoyed me forward;
        and I found myself upright

in the instant, with a garden
    inside my own ribs aflourish. There, the arbor leafs.
        The vines push out plump grapes.
        You are loved, someone said. Take that

and eat it.

Paul J. Willis was born in California in 1955. For more than 25 years, he has been Professor of English at Westmont College, and has recently served as Poet Laureate of Santa Barbara, California. He is a mountaineer, whose essay collection *Bright Shoots of Everlastingness* was published by Word-Farm in 2005. His third poetry collection is *Say This Prayer Into the Past* (Poiema Poetry Series, 2014).

The Good Portion

Mary has chosen the good portion, which shall not be taken away from her. —Luke 10:42

Is it waking to this calm morning
after a night of dry winds?

Is it scrambled eggs, the ones with cheese,
or the hot glaze of a cinnamon roll?

Is it the way you laugh over breakfast,
that generous gift, your laughter?

Is it rinsing the plates and pans in the sink?
Or leaving them in a cockeyed stack,

these things of use, these things of beauty
that will not be taken away?

Rosing from the Dead

We are on our way home
from Good Friday service.
It is dark. It is silent.
"Sunday," says Hanna,
"Jesus will be rosing
from the dead."

It must have been like that.
A white blossom, or maybe
a red one, pulsing
from the floor of the tomb, reaching
round the Easter stone
and levering it aside
with pliant thorns.

The soldiers overcome
with the fragrance,
and Mary at sunrise
mistaking the dawn-dewed
Rose of Sharon
for the untameable Gardener.

Christmas Child

When you were born, sycamore leaves
were brown and falling. They sifted
through the stable door and laid their hands
upon your cheek. Sunlight bent
through cracks in the wall and found
your lips. It was morning now.
Joseph slept, curled on the straw in a corner.

Your mother offered her breast
to you, the warm milk of humankind,
of kindness. You drank from the spongy
flesh as you could, a long way now
from vinegar, but closer, closer,
closer than the night before.

She cradles you, O Jesus Christ,
born in blood and born to bleed,
for this brief dawn a simple child, searching
the nipple, stirring among the whisper,
the touch, of sycamore.

Intercession

When I wake in the night and think
of what I might have said in class that day,
I wonder why my life consists

of inarticulate occasions.
No timely word, only belated ones.
Every hour a first draft, and then another.

It makes me want to announce, "Listen!
Listen to what I do not say. Listen

to what it is you cannot say yourselves."

There are sighs and groans,
          just sighs and groans.
Interpret them, dear ones, as you may.

Listen

A lake lies all alone in its own shape.
It's not going anywhere.

A lake can wait a long time
for a hiker to come
and camp on its shore.

It will reflect the moonlight,
give him a drink of pale silver.

Toward dawn, the wind might ruffle
it a little, and the water
will have words with the granite.

Once the hiker goes away
through October meadows,

the lake will sparkle by itself.
You'll never see it. There is
so much you will never see.

Wood Violet

(*Viola glabella*)

Yellow wood violet,
   I don't deserve you.
      Does anyone?

The way you line
   both sides of the path
      above the creek,

leading upward
   from shade to sun,
      makes me think of you as

ushers to a new redemption.
   Each spring, a second chance.
      And a third. And a fourth.

   —Ross Lake National Recreation Area

Malcolm Guite was born in Ibadan, Nigeria in 1957. He is Chaplain of Girton College in the University of Cambridge, England. His three poetry collections—Sounding the Seasons (2012), The Singing Bowl (2013) and Parable and Paradox (2016)—are all published by Canterbury Press. He often uses traditional poetic forms such as the sonnet.

Prologue: Sounding the Seasons

Tangled in time, we go by hints and guesses,
Turning the wheel of each returning year.
But in the midst of failures and successes
We sometimes glimpse the Love that casts out fear.
Sometimes the heart remembers its own reasons
And beats a *Sanctus* as we sing our story,
Tracing the threads of grace, sounding the seasons
That lead at last through time to timeless glory.
From the first yearning for a Saviour's birth
To the full joy of knowing sins forgiven
We start our journey here on God's good earth
To catch an echo of the choirs of heaven.
I send these out, returning what was lent,
Turning to praise each 'moment's monument'.

O Clavis (*from* The Great O Antiphons)

Even in the darkness where I sit
And huddle in the midst of misery
I can remember freedom, but forget
That every lock must answer to a key,
That each dark clasp, sharp and intricate,
Must find a counter-clasp to meet its guard,
Particular, exact and intimate,
The clutch and catch that meshes with its ward.
I cry out for the key I threw away

That turned and over turned with certain touch
And with the lovely lifting of a latch
Opened my darkness to the light of day.
O come again, come quickly, set me free
Cut to the quick to fit, the master key.

Crucifixion: Jesus is Nailed to the Cross (*from* The Stations of the Cross)

See, as they strip the robe from off his back
And spread his arms and nail them to the cross,
The dark nails pierce him and the sky turns black,
And love is firmly fastened onto loss.
But here a pure change happens. On this tree
Loss becomes gain, death opens into birth.
Here wounding heals and fastening makes free
Earth breathes in heaven, heaven roots in earth.
And here we see the length, the breadth, the height
Where love and hatred meet and love stays true
Where sin meets grace and darkness turns to light
We see what love can bear and be and do,
And here our saviour calls us to his side
His love is free, his arms are open wide.

St Peter

Impulsive master of misunderstanding
You comfort me with all your big mistakes;
Jumping the ship before you make the landing,
Placing the bet before you know the stakes.
I love the way you step out without knowing,
The way you sometimes speak before you think,
The way your broken faith is always growing,
The way he holds you even when you sink.
Born to a world that always tried to shame you,
Your shaky ego vulnerable to shame,
I love the way that Jesus chose to name you,
Before you knew how to deserve that name.
And in the end your Saviour let you prove
That each denial is undone by love.

St Stephen

Witness for Jesus, man of fruitful blood,
Your martyrdom begins and stands for all.
They saw the stones, you saw the face of God,
And sowed a seed that blossomed in St. Paul.
When Saul departed breathing threats and slaughter
He had to pass through that Damascus gate
Where he had held the coats and heard the laughter
As Christ, alive in you, forgave his hate,
And showed him the same light you saw from heaven
And taught him, through his blindness, how to see;
Christ did not ask 'Why were you stoning Stephen?'
But 'Saul, why are you persecuting me?'
Each martyr after you adds to his story,
As clouds of witness shine through clouds of glory.

Benedict

You sought to start a simple school of prayer,
A modest, gentle, moderate attempt,
With nothing made too harsh or hard to bear,
No treating or retreating with contempt,
A little rule, a small obedience
That sets aside, and tills the chosen ground,
Fruitful humility, chosen innocence,
A binding by which freedom might be found

You call us all to live, and see good days,
Centre in Christ and enter in his peace,
To seek his Way amidst our many ways,
Find blessedness in blessing, peace in praise,
To clear and keep for Love a sacred space
That we might be beginners in God's grace.

The Rose (*from* On Reading the Commedia)

A white rose opens in a quiet arbour
Where I sit reading Dante. Paradise
Unfolding in me, opens hour by hour,

In sunlight and amidst the hum of bees
On a late afternoon. I think of how
Everything flowers, the whole universe

Itself is still unfolding even now,
Sprung from a stem of singularity
Which petals time and space. I think of how

The very elements that let my body be
Began and will continue in the stars
Whose light and distance frame our mystery,

And how my shadowed heart still loves, still bears
With every beat that animates my being,
Eternal yearnings through the turning years.

I turn back to the lines that light my seeing
And lift me to the limits of all thought
And long that I might also find that freeing

And enabling Love, and so be caught
And lifted into his renewing Heaven.
Evening glimmers and the stars come out.

Venus is shining clear. My prayers are woven
Into a sounding song, a symphony,
As all creation gives back what is given

In music made to praise the Mystery
Who is both gift and giver. Something stirs
A grace in me beyond my memory.

I close the book and look up at the stars.

Descent

They sought to soar into the skies,
Those classic gods of high renown,
For lofty pride aspires to rise,
But you came down.

You dropped down from the mountains sheer,
Forsook the eagle for the dove,
The other Gods demanded fear,
But you gave love.

Where chiseled marble seemed to freeze

Their abstract and perfected form,
Compassion brought you to your knees,
Your blood was warm.

They called for blood in sacrifice,
Their victims on an altar bled,
When no one else could pay the price,
You died instead.

They towered above our mortal plain,
Dismissed this restless flesh with scorn,
Aloof from birth and death and pain,
But you were born.

Born to these burdens, borne by all
Born with us all 'astride the grave,'
Weak, to be with us when we fall,
And strong to save.

Li-Young Lee was born in Jakarta, Indonesia in 1957, and moved to the US in his childhood. His memoir *The Winged Seed: A Remembrance* (1995) received the American Book Award. He is the author of four poetry collections, including *Behind My Eyes* (Norton, 2008). He and his family live in Chicago.

God Seeks a Destiny

The child climbs into the apple tree
and can't get down,
and can't cry out for fear
he'll wake the baby inside the house.

From where he's perched, he can see into
all the windows at the back of the house.

There's his sister painting her eyelids
the hues of morning and evening.

There's his brother falling asleep
over his ABC's and 1,2,3's.

There's the baby
in a basket beside his mother,
who's seated at the kitchen table.
She's adding and subtracting numbers
in a dog-eared ledger.
And he can tell by her frown she's suspicious
Death owns the figures
and the decimal is a double agent.

And where is his father?
In the room with the shut curtains of course.
He's talking to God again, who plays
hide and seek among His names.

But wasn't it God who lured the child
even higher into the tree with glimpses
of God's own ripening body?

Stranded thus in a branching net
staked between earth and sky, between
present summer and future summer,
isn't the boy god's prey?

And who wakes now but God in the boy's flesh
and astonished bright blood,

as his hands suddenly see,
his feet begins to find
his weight alive,
his mind aligned
not with the fate of a stunned will

but some greener knowing and
feeling his way back to earth.

God's destiny is safe
for now inside the child.

William Jolliff was born in Ohio in 1958, and grew up in the evangelical Quaker tradition. He is an English professor at George Fox University in Oregon, and plays traditional music on the five-string banjo and other Appalachian folk instruments. He is the editor *of The Poetry of John Greenleaf Whittier*. His poetry collection *Twisted Shapes of Light* (2015) is part of the Poiema Poetry Series.

Sermon for a Monday

> *Therefore the Lord God sent him forth from the garden of Eden, to till the ground from whence he was taken.* (Genesis 3:23)

A body grows old, holding all that sadness,
        bearing it like a tumor.
The back bends crooked, offering all that care,
        hunching in accustomed pain.
The trunk twists, spreading heavy branches so wide,
        and the earth beneath turns dry.

The feet and knees that drag the body to work
        race up a hill that needn't be a hill.
The truck chokes and shudders down a gear,
        grieved that it cannot go fast.
A tornado is coming! Hide in the cellar!
        We can live in the musty dark.

Wisdom, being small, demands that we use it,
        those little wisps we've managed to gather.
Two great teachings of our good old brother:
        It is finished. Remember the lilies.
So let's be sad together, weep in the floods
        of all that childhood heartbreak.

Maybe we should rub our faces in pasture grass,
        even though the cows have grazed here.
Maybe we should roll in heaps of crimson leaves,

even though we know the snow comes next.
This world is a sad and hostile place. It is also Paradise.

Dairymen at Prayer Meeting

Their foreheads shone where seed caps curled
above their brows, shadowing eyes
that squinted each day down long rows
of soybeans, fodder corn, turning oats.

Their overalls shone too, bright blue,
when, hard-scrubbed, they came to hear
the Word read aloud, in a tongue they grew
to believe the low-toned dialect of God.

At close they knelt to face the pews
and fold swollen hands that stank
of antiseptic wash, tough and pink,
stiff with milking twice each day

forever. I don't recall a moment's doubt
that the Lord heard every syllable,
a Father God who'd surely known
heartaches, troubles enough of his own:

wind, maybe, when wheat was fit to cut,
a girl gone wrong in the noise of town,
deaf to the warnings of Love's hard voice.
Or that one good son, who died so young.

D.S. Martin was born in Toronto in 1958. His collections include *Poiema* (Wipf & Stock, 2008) and *Conspiracy of Light: Poems Inspired by the Legacy of C.S. Lewis* (Cascade, 2013)—and one chapbook, *So The Moon Would Not Be Swallowed* (Rubicon, 2007). He is Series Editor for the Poiema Poetry Series, and has edited this anthology—which grew out of his blog *Kingdom Poets*.

Lunar Eclipse (June 1928)

Yencheng, Honan, China

On Sunday evening as darkness crept in
the people rushed out
with gongs
    & pots
        & anything to make noise
to scare the heavenly dog
that slowly
    very slowly
        ever so slowly
had placed its jaws about the moon

They persisted in their din   it was said
so the moon would not be swallowed
& leave them in the dark   forever

The Sacrifice of Isaac

God told Abraham   Kill your son for me   & they
climbed Mount Moriah so there would be a great
distance of rock cloud shadow & light to be sliced in
two   & the perplexing covenant might come to mind as
you stare toward the blue horizon

The knife seems to fall forever
as Abraham (looking like an old man Rembrandt
frequently sketched) palms the bound youth's face
with a large determined hand to shield him from the
sight

The knife seems to fall forever
giving you time to think of bloody Passover   of Jesus
as sacrificial lamb   of what kind of god would ask so
much   & what kind of father could do it (as a
windblown angel seizes the old man's wrist)

Then you notice the eyes   bloodshot & observant
of a ram caught in a thicket   This is no happy ending
Three centuries after Rembrandt
the knife still falls

The Humiliation

Like damp mist
freezing on a lamppost
this is the humiliation of myth into fact
the abstract   spilled like blood on concrete
the allusive grown bold
the ritual symbolic act   contracted
from everywhere   to the backside of nowhere
from mystery to history
from the always   down to these particular days

This names a town   a time   a governor
a man & his teen bride   Each lineage is traced
shows how the greatest humiliation took place
of God into Man
Here   the infinite condensed to infant
the eternal was confined   to one instant at a time

The Sacred Fish

You can't desire to catch the sacred fish
as much as he desires to be caught
& yet
he darts through the dim depths
with tail swerve & swish
laughs with the joy of glistening fins
at huge holes in your net
through which he swims

To get the shining coin from his mouth
is worth selling all you have
To get *him*   even better
Everything you know about him
wavers in uneven light

Just below the surface
so it's barely wet
you let down your net
as he dives to the bottom
You seek the depths
as he leaps through waves
You search the shallows
as he heads for open water
& your tattered nets come up empty

If you let him
he'll repair them himself
trim knotted clumps   & untie tangles
Selecting the right fibres
he'll tear & twist
the sinews of your heart into fine mesh
stretch them as thin as a pin
as wide as your whole being
a needle-shimmer piercing your soul

Better is one day in his boats
than thousands elsewhere

Nocturne With Monkey

We are inveterate poets

– C.S. Lewis

Does the capuchin monkey   hanging from his prehensile tail
see the stars   or just a speckled ceiling
beyond the Peruvian jungle's darkening canopy?
When his gathering of palm nuts is hindered
by the approach of creeping night
might he stop to consider those points of light?
Might he   staring into the deep
comprehend their distance
their size   their number   & then wonder
or is his imagination limited to foraging   & wedging
himself in high treetops for his night's sleep?
Might he be overcome with awe   or is the sight
of a shadowy snake or a slinking cat
at the foot of his tree   his only cause of fright?

A man   walking the terraces of night
might be preoccupied with inconsequential things
& not notice the   insufficiently bright
smudge of Andromeda's spiral
on a moonless night
but should he stop   to marvel at the sky's expanse
his considerations measure more than space & time
for numbers are only the foothold   from which
his imagination's leap   thrusts toward the sublime
Might it be his own shadow   the shadow of God's image
stretching across the galaxies   that carries such consequence

since merely seeing such blotches of light
seems to have no teeth   to bite a lesser mind?
We are left   like Pascal   terrified by the silence

Marjorie Maddox was born in 1959. She is Professor of English and Director of Creative Writing at Lock Haven University in Pennsylvania. She is the co-editor of *Common Wealth: Contemporary Poets on Pennsylvania* (2005). Her new, tenth, poetry collection is *True, False, None of the Above* (Poiema Poetry Series, 2016).

Backwards Barn Raising

Nickel Mines, October 2006

And what can we do but wail with you,
grief burning back to ashes,

those splintered schoolroom boards
that heard the bullets?

Flames hot enough to melt the nails—
now and then—

rise up in our eyes; we hear
that ancient hammer thud

echo, "*Eli, Eli,*
lama sabachthani. . ."

Can what is lost be leveled?
You hold each other's hands,

huddle in an unending circle,
". . ..as we forgive those who trespass against us."

Even out of this,
you build forgiveness.

And the Topic for Today is Environmentalism . . . .

Teaching "God's Grandeur"

More politically correct than divine grandeur,
it too flames out in this small Pennsylvania town
where fracking hijacks the headlines. Good reason
and good enough to bring the state students trodding
heavily into a poem piled high with God and earth,
with "responsibilities" they hear each morning
as the gas industry trucks rattle past our windows,
their tired drivers knowing nothing
of iambic pentameter or sestets but much
about food on the table, a steady job.

The freshmen, eager now,
blurt out *dilemma, paradox, instress*—
and all those other new-sounding ideas
suddenly connected to their lives,
their parents, the sonnet
they think was written last week,
even with its 19th century,
sound-packed syllables they don't get
until slowing down, thinking.

And so—after playing with light, foil, sound;
the way trade "sears," "blears," and "smears";
and how and why shoes separate us from ground—
we detour to Genesis, Cat Stevens, and a heavy metal rendition
that almost drowns out Hopkins with bass.
All this before rounding the terrain-raked bend
to solution, which is what—they are surprised to discover—
we all most want: the eloquent octet, the bright wings,
the *ah!* that opens the mind to talk,
at long last, about the holy.

The Fourth Man

His face is the greater flame
but doesn't flicker. No furnace
fuels his glory. "Son of gods,"
the king calls out and cowers from the heat.
Sparks crown our heads.
We are un-singed and sing of seraphs,
genuflect before his servant,
ten times as golden as any man-made
Hades that can't consume
the luminous, the purified,
the once-upon-a-time-burning-bush,
the evermore-ignited blaze
of Yahweh.

Prayer

> *"a flight of the heart towards*
> *the throne of God."*
>
> —*St. Joseph Cafasso*

How the air
of prayer

   breathes and buoys—
   not words,

     not even the slight lift
     of almost-thought, but less/

       more; who can tell
       the teaspoon of light

beneath wings that tilt,
just so, toward eternity?

It is the breeze
of eyelids closing,

the wind
of knees bending,

the mind
without knowing

soaring beyond
what we know of beyond.

Seek and Ye. . . .

"Where there is no love,
put love—and you will find love."

-St. John of the Cross

But where it is—this promise of
reap-after-sow, get-after-give, find-after-look,
cheek-after-turn, rise-after-down, live-after-
-not-happily—where it is
slipped in or slashed open
or stomped on or   Where it is?
Elusive as air, as omniscience, as prayer
trip-tripping these clay feet
indefinitely; one glance of your askance
gaze, and the *un* comes clattering off
conditional just when I begin
hope-against-hope to believe
I can see.

Eric Pankey was born in 1959 in Kansas City, Missouri. His first collection won the Walt Whitman Award in 1984. He has since published many books, including, *The Pear As One Example: New and Selected Poems, 1984—2008* (Ausable Press, 2008). He is Professor of English at George Mason University in Washington.

In Memory

If the world is created from the Word,
What can I hear amid the noise of that one
Assertion and all that rattles and diminishes

In its wake: the mockingbird's trill and grate,
The sluice and overlap where the creek narrows,
The dragonfly needling through the humid air?

And what will I hear when words are no more?
I cannot hear you now, ash-that-you-are,
My beloved, who in your passion and error,

In what was your life gave life to me,
My life from the life of your blunt body
That is no more. If I believe that Christ

Is risen, why can't I believe that we too
Will be risen, rejoined, and relieved
Of the world's tug and the body's ballast?

We are asked to testify, to bear
Witness to what we have seen and heard,
And yet our hope is in the veiled and silenced.

I take comfort in your silence,
In the absence of the voice that voiced your pain.
The body apart from the spirit is dead

But that does not mean the spirit is dead.

In Siena, Prospero Reconsiders
the Marriage at Cana

All sleight-of-hand trails the dross and clutter
Of the unseen, clumsily like an anchor,
Barely concealing its means as it deceives.

What else can be made of signs and wonders
But close readings and a display of awe?
What is left when the waited-upon is fulfilled?

After the standoff Jesus conjures a trick.
Should such an act be enacted knowing
The next and the next will be demanded?

Of course, he one-ups himself, causes a fuss,
And the story plunges headlong to finale.
And then encore. Above, in the Sienese heat,

A pair of ravens patrol the parapet.
Washed linens flap on the clothesline.
A shadow bisects the curved blade of the Campo.

As if in confirmation of a miracle,
The twisted olive bears the wind's history,
A gnarl that hinders the brisk disorder,

Renders it as the unmoved here and now.
Skittish pigeons clatter up in the air.
Into shadow. Out of shadow. And then back down.

And no one, not even God, lifted a finger.

Parable With My Father as a Boy

He woke at an hour the church bells no longer strike.
At that porous border between night and morning,
He gleaned windfall, russet to rose, all pocked and blemished,
And pressed it to a winy, tin-edged cider.
He foraged for seeds and nuts, dug up tubers.
Hung the white-tail from the rafters and slit its throat;
Its blood tick-tocked into a galvanized pail.
All this before his sisters woke and pestered him:
The thaw has come and yet our parents remain unburied!

Where are the eggs? Why has the milk soured?
Is that the Adversary stealing our nanny goat?
Only yesterday, while you napped, he sowed tares in the field!

Richard Greene was born in Newfoundland in 1961. He teaches at the University of Toronto. His collection, *Boxing the Compass*, was awarded the Governor General's Award for poetry in 2010. He has written biographies of the novelist Graham Greene, and the poet Dame Edith Sitwell.

Exultet

A log in its brazier makes sweet smoke at the door:
I think it is cedar, but old Pete says no,
a two-hour log from Canadian Tire.
The long candle is blessed: 'Christ yesterday
and today, the beginning and the end,
alpha and omega, all time belongs to him. . ..'
The priest's vestments begin to ripple
over flames: what if alb, stole, chasuble
light up, and his big frame turns lantern?
The breeze relents; the fabric falls safe.
He gathers flame on a splinter and lifts it
to the candle. At the threshold he chants:
'Christ our Light.' We answer: 'Thanks be to God.'
And the lights go round, taper to taper,
a hundred lit souls in country darkness.

*

I remember Anne Colleen — wide eyes, blonde hair,
a little girl with a card sharp's knack:
knew what lay face down, what was in the deck,
whether ace or deuce was on its way.
The last time I saw her, twenty years on,
was at Carnell's, while her daughter frolicked
with dolls beneath our grandmother's coffin.
This morning I hear of her unlucky inheritance
from that good woman, who made ninety-two
against the odds, clots floating in her veins.
Without warning, Anne Colleen's lungs filled;
emergency medics offered one chance,
an induced coma and thrombolytics to break

the clot. They loosened other hidden clots
that swam straight home, heart attack
after heart attack and she was gone.
That was Good Friday and she was forty-one.

*

A small parish, the choir leader plays deacon
and her voice from the loft trembles
above the little flames: 'Rejoice heavenly powers!
Rejoice choirs of angels!' My mind is elsewhere
though phrases break through: 'Rejoice, O mother church!
Exult in glory! The risen Saviour shines upon you!'
There are all the chances that lie between
my life and hers – my infinite good luck,
health and friends and fortune. For me, love
could not fail for long, which for others
burned down to its unreviving ash
and died; this life of mine passing 'dry-shod
through the sea' – this mystery of gifts.

*

In the front pew, Pete grapples with a book
of hymns, blows out the taper, and applies
both hand and hook to the task. He is the age
to have fought in Korea, and on Remembrance
Day salutes the sad uniform hung to the left
of the altar. He tells us it was not war
but gardening that took his hand, a mulcher
bit it off. I almost wish he had the dignity
of a numbered hill. I think too of the priest
who nearly lost his faith not because
a farmer-friend dropped dead, but because he
fell face down in the mud. Happy fault
or happenstance, the human heart will break
to hear of it. And yet laid side by side,
presence and absence, glory and disarray,
the years give back to grief the sense of light
and there is for most a reason to give thanks.

*

And so it is, I am again a month shy of sixteen,

190

the school-year ending, and everything else
beginning. We circle the clover leafs,
learn to shoulder check and to change lanes
without risk of pile-up. Waiting my turn
in the back seat, I mouth the verses
of a hymn, silent and growing wordless
as they wind downwards to whatever
there is of me, the unmade self. In the nights
of that week, I pray for every soul
I can remember, face by face, rising
out of a boy's memory. By the weekend,
my mind has surrendered to the light
of June. I take communion in an evening
church. As never before or after,
I am given to love and fall from words.

*

Half a lifetime passes, and I stand here on
the night of resurrection, pondering
the 'morning star which never sets' but promises
return: 'Christ that morning star,
who came back from the dead,
and shed his peaceful light on all mankind,' —
a glory bound to littleness and sorrows
in the pietà of the common day.

Julia Spicher Kasdorf was born in 1962—in Lewistown, Pennsylvania—to Mennonite parents who chose to leave their closed, rural community to work in the city. She is Associate Professor of English and women's studies at Pennsylvania State University. Her three poetry books, including *Poetry In America* (2011), are all published by University of Pittsburgh Press.

Green Market, NY

The first day of false spring, I hit the street,
buoyant, my coat open. I could keep walking
and leave that job without cleaning my desk.
At Union Square the country people slouch
by crates of last fall's potatoes.
An Amish lady tends her table of pies.
I ask where her farm is. "Upstate," she says,
"but we moved from P.A. where the land is better,
and the growing season's longer by a month."
I ask where in P.A. "Towns you wouldn't know,
around Mifflinburg, around Belleville."
And I tell her I was born there.
"Now who would your grandparents be?"
"Thomas and Vesta Peachey."
"Well, I was a Peachey," she says,
and she grins like she sees the whole farm
on my face. "What a place your folks had,
down Locust Grove. Do you know my father,
the Harness shop on the Front Mountain Road?"
I do. And then we can't think what to say
that Valley so far from the traffic on Broadway.
I choose a pie while she eyes my short hair
then looks square on my face. She knows
I know better than to pay six dollars for this.
"Do you live in the city?" she asks, "do you like it?"
I say no. And that was no lie, Emma Peachey.
I don't like New York, but sometimes these streets
hold me as hard as we're held by rich earth.

I have not forgotten that Bible verse:
Whoever puts his hand to the plow and looks back
is not fit for the kingdom of God.

Thinking of Certain Mennonite Women

When I think I can't bear to trace
one more sorrow back to its source,
I think of Lois those summer evenings,
when, supper dishes done, she'd climb
a windmill and cling beneath its great blades,
drawing water from under her father's fields.
She'd stay there until the sun went down
on barn roof, garden, and the one paved road
pointing toward town. When I am afraid
to set out once more alone, I see Julie
pumping her legs so hard she believes
she will fly off the swing set and land
gently on the lawn. I see her let go,
braids streaking behind, then see her knees
shredding on gravel, stuck to stockings
each time she kneels to pray at a pew.
When I can't tell my own desire
from the wishes of others, I remember
my mom, too young to know or care better,
flinging her jumper, blouse, socks, and slip
into the wind, dancing for flower beds
until her mother discovers. When I wonder
how I should live this only one life,
I think of how they tell these stories:
honestly, without explanation,
to whoever will listen.

On Leaving Brooklyn

1998

After Psalm 137

If I forget thee
let my tongue forget the songs
it sang in this strange land
and my heart forget the secrets
only a stranger can learn.
Borough of churches, borough of crack,
if I forget how ailanthus trees sprout
on the rooftops, how these streets
end in water and light,
let my eyes grow nearsighted.
Let my blood forget
the map of its travels
and my other blood cease
its slow tug toward the sea
if I do not remember,
if I do not always consider thee
my Babylon, my Jerusalem.

Sometimes It's Easy to Know What I Want

On a road that cuts through the richest, nonirrigated land
in the nation, according to some Lancaster, PA, natives,

a minivan slowed, and a woman with a good haircut yelled,
Do you want a ride, or are you walking because you want to?

I didn't reply because my life felt so wrecked—
no matter the reason, either you get this or you don't—

wrecked in the way that makes gestures of tenderness
devastating, like the time I showed up in Minnesota, brittle

with sorrow, and the professor sent to fetch me
asked if I wanted heat in the seat of his sports car

or the local apple he'd brought in case I arrive hungry.
I didn't know people make seats to hold a body in radiance

like the merciful had of God. The apple was crisp and cold
and sweet. Maybe I looked in his eyes and shook his hand

in both of mine when I left, I don't remember. Months later,
he sent an empty seed packet, torn open, lithographed

with a fat, yellow annual no one grows anymore, flamboyant
as Depression-era glassware. That was all, thank you.

Thank you, oh thank so much, I finally told the woman
framed by a minivan window, but yes, I do want to walk.

Michael Symmons Roberts was born in Preston, England in 1963. His seven poetry collections, including *Selected Poems* (2016), have all been published by Jonathan Cape. In 2006, in conjunction with a BBC television series, he published *The Miracles of Jesus* (Lion-Hudson). He is a librettist, and has also published two novels. He is a Professor at Manchester Metropolitan University.

Jairus

So, God takes your child by the hand
and pulls her from her deathbed.
He says: 'Feed her, she is ravenous.'

You give her fruits with thick hides
– pomegranate, cantaloupe –
food with weight, to keep her here.

You hope that if she eats enough
the light and dust and love
which weave the matrix of her body

will not fray, nor wear so thin
that morning sun breaks through her,
shadowless, complete.

Somehow this reanimation
has cut sharp the fear of death,
the shock of presence. Feed her

roast lamb, egg, unleavened bread:
forget the herbs, she has an aching
fast to break. Sit by her side,

split skins for her so she can gorge,
and notice how the dawn
draws colour to her just-kissed face.

Food for Risen Bodies – II

On that final night, his meal was formal:
lamb with bitter leaves of endive, chervil,
bread with olive oil and jars of wine.

Now on Tiberias' shores he grills
a carp and catfish breakfast on a charcoal fire.
This is not hunger, this is resurrection:

he eats because he can, and wants to
taste the scales, the moist flakes of the sea,
to rub the salt into his wounds.

Compline

Sustainer, who brings days by choice,
who cries with everyone who cries;
who gave it flavour, yet took milk
like any grasping baby does,
who knows the empty want of milk-
by hearing all, all a voice.

Comforter, spirit of solace,
protect the joyful from their dreams
which seed in darkness fears of loss;
show us the beauty that redeems,
make purpose from our aimlessness-
by seeing all, give all a face.

Sally Ito was born in Alberta in 1964. She has served as Writer in Residence at University of Manitoba's Centre for Creative Writing and Oral Culture, and has taught writing for several years at Canadian Mennonite University. She has published one book of short fiction, *Floating Shore*, and three of poetry. Her most-recent poetry collection is *Alert to Glory* (Turnstone, 2011).

Sparrows

Today, He is in the sparrows
in their ruffled ordinariness
on the back fence, picking
at leftover seeds and fruits
of the dead. In winter,
the sparrows bear the burden
of the cold, light as the cross
of their hollow bones, and
from the window, they are,
in the glare of holy every day,
framed and hallowed prayer.

Making Cakes

And Abraham hastened into the tent to Sarah, and said, "Make ready quickly three measures of choice flour, knead it, and make cakes." —Genesis 18:6

The husband commands thus, and she obeys, compliant wife.
Make cakes. Her belly is a cake, flat and unleavened.
All these years, trying. Husband hanging on fool promises.
Taking flour, water, and oil, she kneads and punches.
Slappity slap. Whap, whap, whap. *Make cakes he says*,
she grumbles. For whom? Outside are three strangers,
black shadows from behind the tent flap. She hears their voices
between the whaps and slaps of bread being pounded out,

bread like flesh, bread she will feed to nameless beings
her husband has once again deigned to entertain. Through
the other flap, she sees husband dragging the calf across
the yard. He will slaughter that creature for them, the madman,
always so hasty with the killing. Crazy old coot.
Ah, but she has loved him. Whap, whap, whap.
Who else but a crazy man would stay with her
who cannot bear children? She is finished.
The round, flat cakes are done, waiting to be baked.
And then she hears a voice say, *Where is Sarah?*
She looks up. Why, they know her name!
She thinks and laughs. Laughs at the one her husband believes a god.

On Love and Hell

Love is Hell an old song goes, piped in the crushed gravel tones
of a sot who has known too much of its woe. Lovers who have
met the boot, or booted themselves, know the pain love costs.

Like Dante's Hell, there's a special kind of ring for each earthly affec-
tion –
love turned to jealousy, love turned to rage,
love turned to adultery, love turned to hate.
Deeply fallen into the well of our own disgrace,
we cannot make true *caritas* of God's gift without the rings
of our flesh binding us. There's sometimes too, just plain
hard-heartedness, the *I don't love you anymore* indifference
to sacrifice and giving, even of a god of his very life.

Beneath the cross, commerce and junkets still prevail, and love,
love from up there must look like Hell.

Julie L. Moore was born in New Jersey in 1965. She is an Associate Professor, and Writing Center Director, at Cedarville University in Ohio. Her collections include, *Slipping Out of Bloom* (WordTech Editions, 2010), and *Particular Scandals* (Poiema Poetry Series, 2013). Her chapbook *Election Day* appeared in 2006.

Clifton Gorge

There lives the dearest freshness deep down things . . .
Gerard Manley Hopkins

Balsam floods the woods,
    swathing our senses
like moss swaddles roots and earth.
    Ferns flutter in the shadow
of the wind moving through,
    while we descend into the sanctuary
of the gorge like the sun lowers
    its long beams through the green
lattice of leaves above. We hope
    to hit bottom as the thrush

throws its deep voice across the ravine
    where a woodpecker knocks on a door
of oak and a lip of limestone loosens,
    tumbles down, greets us at the stream,
which even now rips through rock,
    then pools its energy along the banks
where minnows animate
    the ruin, stirring the cup
brimming with revival, their small bodies,
    flashes of hallelujah.

The Painted Lady and the Thistle

The painted lady alights on thistle,
    its winged mosaic aflutter with brilliance

and thirst. Here is Adam again,
    his brow stitched in toil,
his back breaking out in sweat.

    What will the blossom, edged
with thorny predicaments, offer

    as this butterfly plunges
its proboscis into the core
    ablaze with being?

Of course you already know.
    Every sip, a miracle, a curse

that never disappoints the one
    whose instinct is to drink
first, ask questions later.

The Grass Grows Ordinary

It's nine o'clock and the flesh of evening turns
    pink as salmon. My husband calls me to the porch
where we sit, watching our son and his friend,
    their faces aglow with rose,

tossing their blossom-leathered ball.
    Our sidewalk blushes, the lawn dons
rouge. My grandmother died this morning
    just before my grandfather walked

through the door of the nursing home.
      When my aunt arrived, he raised
his coffee cup, said, *Hey, kid, want some?*
      The rest of the family, on the other side

of the country, was still in church.
      So my aunt left us messages,
her words, steeped in grief's briny
      distillation, greeted us as we returned

home. A neighbor's bottle rocket
      whines, shearing the dream-like
fabric of dusk, erupts in green applause,
      then falls silent as a star. Why,

my sister and I will wonder later,
      didn't Grandmom wait
till after her daily lunch with Granddad?
      What, my mom calls to ask, *will you wear*

to the funeral? A car door slams
      in the distance. The light fades in minutes.
Already, the concrete pales, the grass
      grows ordinary in its dark suit.

Remember Blessing

When you see blood run like hell
down car-bombed streets or smell the fire
of guns in your red-brick schools,
when you taste the metal
of unjust war or feel the fields
quake from the screams of children
fettered to the long arm
of a godless law,

when you blink,
hoping you will open your eyes
and all these pictures will have vanished
and the world is actually a good place,
but they don't, and it's not,
when you've lost your faith,

remember blessing.

You will already know sin
is real—how it sucks breath
from the lungs of joy—
and that sometimes, you are guilty.
You will already know pain.
And the evil that mushrooms
when power is at stake.

So remember then
the way you walked through your yard in the summers
of your youth, searching for the only treasure
within reach, a star glittering on the blushing
face of quartz, sun tapping stone
with its magic wand.

Remember the way the soil felt on your fingertips as you dug in.

Remember the ant toting its nugget toward its hill,
the grasshopper leaping
onto your lap, the worm's nose
rising into the air, as if to sniff your skin.

Remember your brother, or your sister, close by,
digging, too, the dirt's musky aroma,
your sweat, and the moment of discovery,
lifting the pink fingerprint
of God from the earth.

Martha Serpas was born in Galliano, Louisiana in 1965. Her third poetry collection, *The Diener* (2015) was published by LSU Press. She is a Professor of English at the University of Houston, in Texas, and has also worked as a trauma hospital chaplain.

As If There Were Only One

In the morning God pulled me onto the porch,
a rain-washed gray and brilliant shore.

I sat in my orange pajamas and waited.
God said, "Look at the tree." And I did.

Its leaves were newly yellow and green,
slick and bright, and so alive it hurt

to take the colors in. My pupils grew
hungry and wide against my will.

God said, "Listen to the tree."
And I did. It said, "Live!"

And it opened itself wider, not with desire,
but the way I imagine a surgeon spreads

the ribs of a patient in distress and rubs
her paralyzed heart, only this tree parted

its own limbs toward the sky—I was the light in that sky.
I reached in to the thick, sweet core

and I lifted it to my mouth and held it there
for a long time until I tasted the word

tree (because I had forgotten its name).
Then I said my own name twice softly.

Augustine said, God loves each of us as if
there were only one of us, but I hadn't believed him.

And God put me down on the steps with my coffee
and my cigarettes. And, although I still

could not eat nor sleep, that evening
and that morning were my first day back.

The Diener

We hated the early anatomists
for showing us how fragile we are,
how God's image is composite:
the liver the bright bruise of a sunset,
the thyroid wrapped around our throats
for luck. They saw our brains folded
against our foreheads and knew our hearts
pump dumbly on through the wash.
And wily guts take the brunt of it,
pushing to get rid of while we insist
on taking in and taking in and taking in.
Theirs was heresy, that is, a choice
to reach the Artist by testing the art,
human suffering always the requisite cost.

Change, what keeps all of it the same,
the Teacher says, no new thing
under the sun. What we make, let's make old
instead, older than the first tool,
which smelled much like the body—
the first blacksmith must have thought—
not quite like displaced blood, but blood at home
in its place among other parts in their places,
and that must be how we began to confuse

the power to examine and change
with the power to create, to be discrete agents,
why we like to see ourselves as whole,
despite the diener piling legs on a cot,
despite the pruned artery, tied and cut.

Badlands

All over his body wolves send up a mad
        chorus to the moon

seeping green
        across his arms and his chest

and where his new liver floats up in him
        like a mushroom's flat cap.

"I feel like I'm tripping," he says
        at a pitch lower than his wife hears

and then "and I don't believe in God."
        No room in that room.

So much white. So much blue.
        The wolves cry the great name

into the hallway where a gurney
        rolls up and down the tile

looking for someone to play catch with.
        Push the wheels straight, pull the cot—

It's my job to take the heat of belief.
On Wednesday

the nurses line up for ashes
            in their white Crocs

and Reeboks. Wolfman
wants God so bad

he tattoos not-God—what seems not-God—
            on his skin, wants to tell me

he's afraid, that the room squeezes
            time like flexible hose,

that he forgets his wife's voice,
            that men come in the night

to argue with him about the nature
            of stars. There are puddles of stars above

the silver wolves on his chest. Not-God sets
            a chair near his bed.

He says thank you and lays
            a hand on the skinny arm

and with his moist stare and rough
            face tries to convey

how much he trusts the moon
            who centers the persistent stars

and how he forgets the soldier sun
            who keeps everyone blinking and quiet.

Christian Wiman was born in west Texas in 1966. He served as the editor of the highly-influential magazine *Poetry* from 2003 to 2013, and has published two books of essays. His fourth poetry collection is *Out In The West* (Farrar, Straus and Giroux, 2014). He now teaches at Yale Institute of Sacred Music and Yale Divinity School.

Every Riven Thing

God goes, belonging to every riven thing he's made
sing his being simply by being
the thing it is:
stone and tree and sky,
man who sees and sings and wonders why

God goes. Belonging, to every riven thing he's made,
means a storm of peace.
Think of the atoms inside the stone.
Think of the man who sits alone
trying to will himself into the stillness where

God goes belonging. To every riven thing he's made
there is given one shade
shaped exactly to the thing itself:
under the tree a darker tree;
under the man the only man to see

God goes belonging to every riven thing. He's made
the things that bring him near,
made the mind that makes him go.
A part of what man knows,
apart from what man knows,

God goes belonging to every riven thing he's made.

This Mind of Dying

God let me give you now this mind of dying
fevering me back
into consciousness of all I lack
and of that consciousness becoming proud:

>   *There are keener griefs than God.*
>   *They come quietly, and in plain daylight,*
>   *leaving us with nothing, and the means to feel it.*

My God my grief forgive my grief tamed in language
to a fear that I can bear.
Make of my anguish
more than I can make. Lord, hear my prayer.

When The Time's Toxins

When the time's toxins
have seeped into every cell
and like a salted plot
from which all rain, all green, are gone
I and life are leached
of meaning
somehow a seed
of belief
sprouts the instant
I acknowledge it:
little weedy hardy would-be
greenness
tugged upward
by light
while deep within
roots like talons
are taking hold again
of this our only earth.

Coming Into The Kingdom

Coming into the kingdom
I was like a man grown old in banishment,
a creature of hearsay and habit, prayerless, porous, a survivor of my-
self.
Coming into the kingdom
I was like a man stealing into freedom when the tyrant dies,
if freedom is freedom where there are no eyes to obstruct it,
if the cold desert and the hard crossing were still regions of me.
I remember unremembered mountains, unspeakable weeds,
a million scents and sights I did not recognize
though they flowed through me like a land I inhabited long before
belonging or
    belief.
Coming into the kingdom
I was like a man who imagines a city in flames and a city at peace
and sets out not knowing whether his homecoming
will be cause for sorrow or rejoicing,
or if indeed there will be one soul that knows him,
or if he is even the same assemblage of cells this side of exile,
or if exile is no longer what he once entered but what he is.
I tried to cry out in the old way
of thanksgiving, ritual lamentation, rockshriek of joy.
There was no answer. Had there ever been?
Remembering it now I do not remember
the arduous journey that must have rendered me a beast,
nor the broad gates opening at the last,
nor the children gathering around me in wonder,
nor the slow reclamation of a life I had been so long denied,
the million instants of exile told in tears.
Coming into the kingdom
I came into the damp and dirtlight of late November in north Chicago,
where the water-lunged bus chuffs and lumbers up Montrose,
and Butch's back gate's broken latch is impervious to curses,
and wires crisscross the alley like a random rune,
and an airplane splits and sutures the blue as it roars for elsewhere.

Witness

Typically cryptic, God said three weasels
slipping electric over the rocks
one current conducting them up the tree
by the river in the woods in the country
into which I walked
away and away and away;
and a moon-blued, cloud-strewn night sky
like an x-ray
with here a mass and there a mass
and everywhere a mass;
and to the tune of a two-year-old
storm of atoms
elliptically, electrically alive—
I will love you in the summertime, Daddy.
I will love you. . .in the summertime.
Once in the west I lay down dying
to see something other than the dying stars
so singularly clear, so unassailably there,
they made me reach for something other.
I said I will not bow down again
to the numinous ruins.
I said I will not violate my silence with prayer.
I said Lord, Lord
in the speechless way of things
that bear years, and hard weather, and witness.

Anya Krugovoy Silver was born in 1968. She teaches English at Mercer University in Macon, Georgia. She has had to struggle against a rare form of breast cancer, which is—at last report—in remission. She received the Georgia Author of the Year Award for her second book—*I Watched You Disappear*. Her third poetry collection is called *From Nothing* (LSU Press, 2016).

Persimmon

I place you by my window so your skin can receive the setting sun,
so your flesh will yield to succulence, lush with juice,
so the saints of autumn will bless your flaming fruit.

Because cancer has left me tired.

Because when I visit God's houses, I enter and leave alone.
Not even in the melting beeswax and swinging musk of incense
has God visited me, not when I've bowed or kneeled or sung.

Because I have found God, instead, when I've crouched in bathrooms,
lain back for the burning of my skin, covered my face and cursed.

Persimmon: votive candle at the icon of my kitchen window,
your four-petaled stem the eye of God in the Temple's dome,
tabernacle of pulp and seed,
dwelling place for my wandering prayers,

I am learning from you how to praise.

Because when your body bruises and softens, you are perfected.
Because your soul, persimmon, is sugar.

Stage IV

Suddenly, gloved hands empty the rooms
of my house, and I'm told
to take only what I can carry.

Faces turn away from me—I'm taboo, now—
the boat I'm set inside is crowded
with others like myself—

they come from their own cities.
Cautiously, we take each other's hands
and trade stories. We learn

of the lucky few who return—
who are able to cross back over.
And in time, their shame

comes to be known as victory.
We use words that once embarrassed
us—courage, prayer, miracle.

And always, we long for our old homes—
we draw scarves over our faces when we weep,
singing the songs of our ancestors.

In this exile, no pillar of dust and fire guides us.
Our passports have been stamped—
our wrists and collarbones have been marked.

Even when the old promises begin to fall away—
when we see less clearly the gardens
of our former lands—still, we are together, friends.

We know what our beloveds do not
yet know. We see through each other
to the lapping silence beyond the Milky Way.

No, it's not

The body of Christ, the priest murmurs,
placing a morsel of bread in my palm.
Only I hear my son whisper, *No, it's not*.
Eight year old skeptic, creed-smasher,
how to stop the erosion of what's possible?
Or unhook faith from what can be seen?

One evening, strolling the Jersey bay,
we took flailing horseshoe crabs
by their spiny tails, tossing them into tides
so they could glide back to the deep sea.
And wasn't that impulse, to save the ugly,
Love? My doubter, miracle-denier,
may God hurl your spikey edges into the waves.
May you be cradled in His body forever.

From Nothing

> *"I am re-begot / Of absence, darkness, death; things which are not."*
>
> –John Donne, "A Nocturnal upon St. Lucy's Day"

Again and again, from nothingness I'm born.
Each death I witness makes me more my own.
     I imagine each excess line of mine erased,
     each muscle shredded, each bone sheared.
      One day, my spine's long spar will snap,
ribs tumbling loose; my face will droop and drop.
Then I'll be re-begot—the air will shimmer
and my molecules will vault, emerging free.
From darkening days, the light will surge and flee.

Mary Szybist was born in Williamsport, Pennsylvania in 1970. She has published two poetry collections, *Granted* (Alice James, 2003) and *Incarnadine* (Graywolf, 2013) —a series of poems inspired by paintings of the Annunciation— which won the National Book Award. She teaches at Lewis & Clark College in Portland, Oregon.

The Cathars Etc.

loved the spirit most
so to remind them of the ways of the flesh,
those of the old god

took one hundred prisoners and cut off
each nose
each pair of lips

and scooped out each eye

until just one eye on one man was left
to lead them home.

People did that, I say to myself,

a human hand lopping at a man's nose
over and over with a dull blade

that could not then slice
the lips clean
but like an old can opener, pushed
into skin, sawed
the soft edges, working each lip

slowly off as
both men heavily, intimately
breathed.

My brave believer, in my private re-enactments,
you are one of them.

I pick up in the aftermath where you're being led
by rope
by the one with the one good eye.

I'm one of the women at the edge of the hill
watching you stagger magnificently,
unsteadily back.

All your faces are tender with holes
starting to darken and scab
and I don't understand how you could
believe in anything that much
that is not me.

The man with the eye pulls you
forward. You're in the square now.
The women are hysterical,
the men are making terrible sounds
from unclosable mouths.

And I don't know if I can do it, if I can touch
a lipless face that might
lean down, instinctively,
to try to kiss me.

White rays are falling through the clouds.
You are holding that imbecile rope.
You are waiting to be claimed.

What do I love more than this
image of myself?

There I am in the square walking toward you
calling you out by name.

Girls Overheard While Assembling a Puzzle

Are you sure this blue is the same as the
blue over there? This wall's like the
bottom of a pool, its
color I mean. I need a
darker two-piece this summer, the kind with
elastic at the waist so it actually
fits. I can't
find her hands. Where does this gold
go? It's like the angel's giving
her a little piece of honeycomb to eat.
I don't see why God doesn't
just come down and
kiss her himself. This is the red of that
lipstick we saw at the
mall. This piece of her
neck could fit into the light part
of the sky. I think this is a
piece of water. What kind of
queen? You mean
right here? And are we supposed to believe
she can suddenly
talk angel? Who thought this stuff
up? I wish I had a
velvet bikini. That flower's the color of the
veins in my grandmother's hands. I
wish we could
walk into that garden and pick an
X-ray to float on.
Yeah. I do too. I'd say a
zillion yeses to anyone for that.

Tania Runyan was born in Long Beach, California in 1972, but now lives in Illinois. She is the author of such collections as *A Thousand Vessels* (Word-Farm, 2011), and *Second Sky* (Poiema Poetry Series, 2013). She has also released two new books from T.S. Poetry Press: *How to Read a Poem* (2014), and *How to Write a Poem* (2015).

The Empty Tomb

John 20

That *woman* was the first word spoken
must have taken even the angels by surprise,

who were used to bringing their fiery glory
down to the clanging swords of battlefields,

to priests tugging at their beards
in lamentation, to voices thundering in temples

and muscles hefting stones from mountaintops,
not to a trembling woman whose hair clung

to her neck with tears, who for a moment
held the souls of the nations like a basket of figs.

El Train Magnificat

Just when I think I've entered my rest
the dull glare of the office two blocks behind me,
a woman under the Wells Street tracks
opens her arms and shouts, *Lord, I thank you!*
Her massive breasts quake in a gray T-shirt;
a sprig of hair trembles in a rubber band.
You made me! I'm here! I'm here!

The metallic rumble of the Green Line
can't drown her voice. She swings her hips,
clapping to the rhythm. I cross through a line of taxis
to avoid her. Now she is turning in grand circles,
her face lifted toward the tracks.
Thank you, thank you, Lord of mine.
I hum to myself, count sidewalk squares, anything
to escape the eye of her swirl. I quicken my stride
around the corner of Madison, until her voice is nothing
but a drift in the storm of buses and horns.
Yet at night, in the cool hour of unrest,
I feel her words rumbling through me
in a constant loop—*I thank you, Lord;*
I thank you, Lord— sparks flickering along my bones,
singeing the edges of my silent life.

Setting My Mind

—driving home from Pekin, IL

Col. 3:2

Salt spews from a cavalcade of trucks,
but still the icy shoulders of the road advance.
I maneuver my minivan over a licorice stick of asphalt.

My family laughs about the Abominable Snowman
stomping up I-55 and toppling
a truck-stop Dairy Queen.

I try to fight my imagining mind:
a bamboo foot-bridge sways over a river,
a quarter-inch slip and plunge into white.

They've taken the side of the storm,

this morning's Doppler watercolor
now a miracle birth in our headlights.

I pray that I can unclench and love,
find the mysteries of the Spirit
in swaths of black ice, the arms

of Christ in the muscled mounds of snow.
The exits count down toward home.
We're safe, I say, *we're safe, I'm safe.*

The kids trace their names in the foggy glass,
flakes like alyssum flowers
blurring their faces in the window.

Put On the New Self

    Col. 3:10

Twenty-five years after Praying the Prayer,
when my new life was supposed to snap in place
like elastic, the smell of crisp, store-rack cotton
propelling me to run with endurance
toward a finish line I could not see,

I lie on the couch with a sour-smelling terrier
curled in the crook of my leg. Today
I will bathe him, punch through three K-cups,
run a trumpet book to the grammar school.
No martyrdom here, no preaching in the streets,
though tomorrow I might plant another bag of daffodils
so in April I can kneel in the gold
and thank All Things New once more.

But now I turn my eyes to things above

in the window, squirrels gibbering in the canopy
of my backyard maple. I doze and wake
to their claws skittering down the trunk,
mentally etch the face of Christ in the bark.

He doesn't need me. He wants me.
Neither Jew nor Greek, male nor female, tired
nor on fire. I will slip into newness again,
fluff the shaking, sodden dog in His name
as He drapes me with his soft and silent weaving.

That Your Love May Abound

> *—the woman down the street*
>
> *Phil. 1:9*

It's hard to love the rusted camper shell,
petunias wilting in old kitchen sinks.

So I go in your skin, woman smoking on the front stoop
with a matted dog roped to the tree.

I wear your calluses that snag the drapes
and scrape your children's hands you hold

when your husband rips the door off the hinges.
I wear the burned-out leather beneath your eyes

aching from staring at foreclosure papers
and feel the relief of dozing off

in the afternoon wrapped in the fleece of whiskey.
When I see the stalagmites of bottles

in your recycling bin, I run my fingers
over the scars on your arms—

rough but stippled with rose and light
like sunrise in the Badlands.

Before All Things

Col. 1:17

The day Christ died a record-long freight train
barreled through the Rollins Road crossing.
For seven minutes tankers and lumber flats
vibrated through the spikes in his wrists.

A fisherman dropped his pole by the retention pond
and headed toward the hill. A girl at a bus stop
clutched her side as the embryo implanted himself.
We'll be late for the movie, I said.

That night, a meteor lit a tongue of fire
over the Midwestern sky. Our kitchen flashed,
and you froze at the sink. *Christ was just born,*
you said. I ground my best coffee as an offering

and kept watch through the night. Legion roared
through the maple leaves; the Pharisees' stones
thudded to the ground. The loaves in the kitchen
ruptured their bags, then the Earth burst into being.

Dave Harrity was born in 1981. An assistant professor of English at Campbellsville University, the recipient of an Emerging Artist Award from the Kentucky Arts Council, he is the author of the craft and spirituality manual *Making Manifest: On Faith, Creativity, and the Kingdom at Hand* (Seedbed, 2013) and two collections, including: *These Intricacies* (Poiema Poetry Series/Cascade Books, 2015).

On Prayer #1

Who walks away holding the pieces of my life?
Are these petitions signs of desire or disease?
Will they ever grow into something I can touch?

A darkness, a trumpet, a tempest, a fire—
ingredients with hope to make an easier belief.
No—simply moving pieces of my life.

And what comes of all these prayers?
Gales of whispers ransoming release—
acceptable necessities, never needing touch.

What I make in darkness despises light so much,
a doubt refusing, a doubt against the one who speaks.
Can I walk away with any peace in my life?

Set aside the scripts—piecemeal voice,
guilt's dusty hands brushed clean.
I want my prayer to be close to touch.

Lord, divide my simple words and see—
shake promises, mistake my awe for reverence.
I'm stepping back cradling the pieces of my life,
but will you become a body I can touch?

After Chuck's Zen Garden

Dawn: The kitchen window beads with rain and you can hear the wind
shouldering the broadside of the house. You look through your win-
dow to Chuck's yard where water and air have washed over his grass,
his trees, his garden, his little pond. It occurs to you that if Chuck were
a Buddhist monk he'd have been up hours ago. But Chuck isn't Bud-
dhist, he's Baptist—he's middle-aged and kind, fleshy and round. He
isn't into tangling his legs like a lotus, or centering his breath with gen-
tle ohhhhhmmmms. And he may or may not be disciplined enough
to be still in the rain hours before sunrise. In fact, his fundamentalism
might cause him to frown upon the thought of it, and your ecumeni-
cal treatment of his well-planned garden. Instead, Chuck only knows
one Noble Truth: *I plant it and God does the rest* he says each time
you compliment his grinning tiger lilies, the velvet tufts of starlight
moss, and frilly softball-sized chrysanthemums. And maybe he's right,
maybe he does nothing. Sometimes it's what you don't do he says.
You think, now, watching his garden soaked with water that the beds
have bloomed because he stayed away. He lets them have the things
they want—whiskered light, nutrient soil, and—most easily—a little
time. Then your mind snaps, you realize you're anxious, expendable,
one needle on Chuck's stoic pine. You sit down at the kitchen table
and everything has meaning in its ability to end. You note the music
in the wind, the clock behind you counting down each dim second.
The world goes on so easily without you. Everything goes on without
you—tectonics, volcanic spews, shifting tide, glacial till. Whatever hap-
pens now, even as it happens slowly as a growing thumbnail, has one
thing in common: the absence of you. Cities get built and babies get
born. Light still makes shadow. And so what? The punchline please:
the pressure's off; enjoy your day. You look at the rugged stones around
the pond in disbelief, the green shafts of soaked flowers, solid like the
spokes in a wheel. You thumb your nose and laugh. You smirk—world
full circle, laid out like a keen, smiling gift.

Jae Newman was born in South Korea in 1982. Unnamed at birth, he was adopted and raised by an American family. He teaches at St. Paul Lutheran School and Northeastern Seminary. His first book, *Collage of Seoul* (2015) is part of the Poiema Poetry Series. He lives in Rochester with his wife and children.

Apartment Near Airport

Soft words folded into envelopes of prayer.
The dogs hear it first.

Not my prayer, but the sound
of shadows in the neighboring trees.

I can feel the shadow of the engine
before I hear it.

Body at rest, I wrestle with God,
nurse wounds in the dark.

Bracing for the heavy presence of the plane,
I cringe in its sound, crawl out

holding wings while steel hips rust
to reveal a man who was never a child,

a man who wanders airports alone at night
attracted to the ebb and flow of runways,

where beneath the grindings of identity,
there's comfort in the fading echo,

the tail of the plane vanishing
into layers of mysterious clouds.

Unnamed

To know you never named me is to know
why I must name my life away in words, in waiting.

 I went to the library, one day, and traced a peninsula,
Korea, into my sketch book.

I wonder if, later, you ever picked a name for me
while doing household chores,

hanging clothes along the Han River shore, or maybe
walking home from the port

with a bag full of fish, and soap
to wash your hands of burying my name in dirt.

Canticle

If I handed you everything, my life
in colorless newspaper font,

and asked you to dip it in papier-mâché
made of paint, mercury, saliva, and glue,

would you, a stranger, be my Samaritan
and layer thin dripping strips

upon this miraculous breath of mine?
Guarding a balloon with closed lips, if

I am called to speak now, friend,
can I trust you? O Lord

I have asked and received so many times,
I forget he cannot turn to you who cannot hear

the dark song that needs no introduction.
Perhaps, only the quiet one among friends,

the one who stays in at night,
can watch the glow of heavenly optics moving

through space, lucid music colliding now
with the echo of a single word you know

but won't say.

Acknowledgements

The Editor would like to acknowledge the support of Imago in bringing this anthology to publication, and the generosity of the following patrons: Incarnation Ministries, Attrell Toyota Scion, Jim & Linda Finn, and Marilyn & Kenneth Fox, as well as the kind support of several other donors.

This anthology would not have been possible without the encouragement of so many of the included poets, several of whom negotiated on my behalf with their publishers. Grateful acknowledgement is made for permission to reprint previously published poems:

Cliff Ashby: "Latter Day Psalms" is from *Plain Song: Collected Poems* (1992). Reprinted with permission of Annabella Ashby.

Margaret Avison: All poems are from The *Collected Poems: Always Now,* by Margaret Avison, and are reprinted with permission from Joan Eichner and The Porcupine's Quill.

Jill Peláez Baumgaertner: "My God, My God" first appeared in *Vineyards*, and "Grace" first appeared in *Priscilla Papers*. All poems are reprinted with permission from the poet, and are from *What Cannot Be Fixed* — Poiema Poetry Series/Cascade Books — © 2014 by Jill Peláez Baumgaertner.

Wendell Berry: "The Way of Pain," The Peace of Wild Things," and "The Wish to Be Generous" are copyright © 2012 by Wendell Berry, from *New Collected Poems*. Reprinted by permission from Counterpoint. All other poems are copyright © 2013 by Wendell Berry, from *This Day: Collected and New Sabbath Poems*. Reprinted by permission from Counterpoint.

Scott Cairns: All poems are reprinted with permission from the poet. Poems taken from *Slow Pilgrim: The Collected Poems* by Scott Cairns, (Brewster, MA: Paraclete Press, 2015). Copyright © 2015 by Scott Cairns. Reprinted with permission from Paraclete Press. "Possible Answers To Prayer" and "Idiot Psalm 1" first appeared in *Poetry*. "Jonah's Imprisonment" first appeared in *Image*. "Parable" first appeared in *Prairie Schooner*.

Kelly Cherry: "Gethsemane" first appeared in *The Atlantic Monthly*. All poems are reprinted with permission from the poet and Louisiana State University Press.

Robert Cording: All poems are reprinted with permission from the poet, and are from *A Word in My Mouth* — Poiema Poetry Series/Cascade Books — © 2013 by Robert Cording.

Barbara Crooker: All poems are reprinted with permission from the poet. «All That Is Glorious Around Us» won the WB Yeats Society of NY's Poetry Prize, and is from *Radiance* (Word Press, 2005). «Sanctus» first appeared in *Rock & Sling* and is from *More* (2010, C&R Press). "Late Prayer" first appeared in *The Cresset* and is from *Gold* — Poiema Poetry Series/Cascade Books — © 2013 by Barbara Crooker. «Passerines» first appeared in *The 55 Project* and is from *Small Rain* (2014, Purple Flag). "The Book of Kells: Chi Rho" first appeared in *In Touch*, and "On Reading Charles Wright on a Fall Afternoon" first appeared in *Kentucky Review*.

Brad Davis: All poems are reprinted with permission from the poet. "After a Snowfall" is from *Opening King David* — Wipf and Stock © 2011 by Brad Davis. "What I Answered" first appeared in *Anglican Theological Review*, "Still Working It Out" first appeared in *Image*, and "Vocation" first appeared in *Spiritus*. These poems are from *Still Working It Out* — Poiema Poetry Series/Cascade Books — © 2014 by Brad Davis.

John F. Deane: All poems are reprinted with permission from the poet. "Name and Nature" first appeared in *Image*. All other poems are from *Snow Falling On Chestnut Hill: New and Selected Poems*, copyright © 2012. Reprinted with permission of Carcanet Press Ltd.

Madeline DeFrees: "Psalm for a New Nun" from *When Sky Lets Go.* Copyright © 1978 by Madeline DeFrees. Reprinted with the permission of George Braziller , Inc., www.georgebraziller.com. "Skid Row" from *Blue Dusk: New and Selected Poems* 1951—2001. Copyright © 2001 by Madeline DeFrees. Reprinted with the permission of The Permissions Company, Inc., on behalf of Copper Canyon Press, www. coppercanyonpress.org. "The Eye" from *Spectral Waves: New and Uncollected Poems.* Copyright © 2006 by Madeline DeFrees. Reprinted with the permission of The PermissionsCompany, Inc., on behalf of Copper Canyon Press, www.coppercanyonpress.org.

B.H. Fairchild: "The Deposition" and "The Problem" are from *Early Occult Memory Systems of the Lower Midwest: Poems.* Copyright © 2003 by B.H. Fairchild. Used by permission of W.W. Norton and Company, Inc.

David Gascoyne: From *New Collected Poems* (2014). Reprinted with permission of Enitharmon Press.

Dana Gioia: All poems are reprinted with permission from the poet.

Richard Greene: "Exultet" from *Dante's House* published by Signal Editions/Véhicule Press is reprinted with the permission of the author and the publisher.

Malcolm Guite: All poems are reprinted with permission from the poet, and are from his collection *Sounding the Seasons*. Reprinted with permission of Canterbury Press.

Dave Harrity: "On Prayer #1" first appeared in *In Touch*, and "After Chuck's Zen Garden" first appeared in *Riverwind*. These poems are reprinted with permission from the poet, and are from *These Intricacies* — Poiema Poetry Series/Cascade Books — © 2015 by Dave Harrity.

Sally Ito: All poems are reprinted with permission from the poet. © 2011 Sally Ito, reprinted by permission from Alert to Glory, Turnstone Press (Winnipeg, MB).

Mark Jarman: All poems are reprinted with permission from the poet. "Unholy Sonnet #22" first appeared in *New Letters*. "Unholy Sonnet

#28" first appeared in *Prairie Schooner*. "At The Communion Rail" first appeared in *Rattle*. Other than "After The Scourging," they are all from *Bone Fires: New and Selected Poems* (2011). "Prayer For Our Daughters" which first appeared in *The New Criterion* is reprinted with permission from Sarabande Books.

Rod Jellema: All poems are reprinted with permission from the poet. "Letter to Lewis Smedes about God's Presence," "We Used to Grade God's Sunsets from the Lost Valley Beach" and "Take a Chance" are from *Incarnality: The Collected Poems of Rod Jellema* (Eerdmans) ©2010, Rod Jellema.

Elizabeth Jennings: All poems are from *The Collected Poems* by Elizabeth Jennings (Carcanet Press) and are reprinted with permission of David Higham Associates.

William Jolliff: These poems are reprinted with permission from the poet, and are from *Twisted Shapes of Light* — Poiema Poetry Series/ Cascade Books — © 2015 by William Jolliff.

Mary Karr: All poems are from *Sinners Welcome* © 2006 by Mary Karr, are published with permission from the poet, from HarperCollins, and from International Creative Management.

Julia Spicher Kasdorf: "Green Market, New York" from *Sleeping Preacher*, by Julia Kasdorf ©1992. Reprinted by permission of University of Pittsburgh Press. "Thinking of Certain Mennonite Women" and "On Leaving Brooklyn" from *Eve's Striptease*, by Julia Kasdorf ©1998. Reprinted by permission of University of Pittsburgh Press. "Sometimes It's Easy to Know What I Want" from *Poetry in America*, by Julia Spicher Kasdorf ©2011. Reprinted by permission of University of Pittsburgh Press.

Sarah Klassen: All poems are reprinted with permission from the poet. "In The Garden" and "Credo" are © 2012 Sarah Klassen, reprinted by permission from *Monstrance*, Turnstone Press (Winnipeg, MB). from Monstrance (2012). "The First Day Of Creation" and "Ritual" both first appeared in *The Christian Century*. "Horizon" is from *Violence And Mercy* (Netherlandic Press, 1991).

Laurie Klein: "The Back Forty" first appeared in *Ascent*. All poems are reprinted with permission from the poet, and are from *Where The Sky Opens*— Poiema Poetry Series/Cascade Books — © 2015 by Laurie Klein.

Andrew Lansdown: All poems are reprinted with permission from the poet. "Prayer," "Kangaroos" and "Black Bamboo" are from *Far From Home: Poems of Faith, Grief and Gladness* (2012, Rhiza Press).

Sydney Lea: All poems are reprinted with permission from the poet. "The Pastor," "Through a Window" and "Barnet Hill Brook" first appeared in *The Christian Century*. "Barnet Hill Brook" is from *Six Sundays Toward a Seventh* — Poiema Poetry Series/Cascade Books — © 2012 by Sydney Lea. «I Was Thinking Of Beauty» is from *I Was Thinking Of Beauty* (Four Way Books) © 2013 by Sydney Lea. "The Pastor" is from *No Doubt The Nameless* (Four Way Books) © 2016 by Sydney Lea.

John Leax: All poems are reprinted with permission from the poet. "Faith in a Seed" by John Leax. Copyright © 2012 by Melissa Stevens. Published in *Recluse Freedom* (WordFarm, 2012). Used with permission from WordFarm. The last six poems are from *Remembering Jesus: Sonnets and Songs* — Poiema Poetry Series/Cascade Books — © 2014 by John Leax.

Li-Young Lee: "God Seeks a Destiny" is reprinted with permission of W.W. Norton and Company, Inc. — © 2008 by Li-Young Lee.

Marjorie Maddox: All poems are reprinted with permission from the poet. "Backwards Barn Raising" is from *Local New From Someplace Else* — Wipf and Stock © 2013 by Marjorie Maddox — and first appeared in the same. All other poems — including "The Fourth Man" which first appeared in *Dappled Things*, "Prayer" which first appeared in *Anglican Theological Review* in a slightly different form, and "The Topic for Today is Environmentalism" which also appeared in *Every Day Poems* — are from *True, False, None of the Above* — Poiema Poetry Series/Cascade Books — © 2016 by Marjorie Maddox.

Paul Mariani: All poems are reprinted with permission from the poet, and are from *Epitaphs for the Journey: New, Selected and Revised Poems* — Poiema Poetry Series/Cascade Books — © 2012 by Paul Mariani.

D.S. Martin: All poems are reprinted with permission from the poet. "Lunar Eclipse (June 1928)," which first appeared in *Windsor Review*, and "The Sacrifice of Isaac," which first appeared in *Christianity & Literature*, are from *Poiema* — Wipf and Stock Publishers — © 2008 by D.S. Martin. "The Humiliation," which first appeared in *Sehnsucht*, "The Sacred Fish," which first appeared in *Sojourners*, and "Nocturne With Monkey," which first appeared in *Anglican Theological Review*, are from *Conspiracy of Light: Poems Inspired by the Legacy of C.S. Lewis* — Poiema Poetry Series/Cascade Books — © 2013 by D.S. Martin.

Walt McDonald: Both poems are from *Faith is a Radical Master: New and Selected Poems* by Walt McDonald. Reprinted with permission of Abilene Christian University Press.

Julie L. Moore: "The Painted Lady and the Thistle" first appeared in *Pirene's Fountain*, "Clifton Gorge" first appeared in *American Poetry Journal* (and later in both *Verse Daily* and *Poetry Daily*), "The Grass Grows Ordinary" first appeared in *Conte: A Journal of Narrative Writing*, and "Remember Blessing" first appeared in *Atlanta Review*. All poems are reprinted with permission from the poet, and are from *Particular Scandals* — Poiema Poetry Series/Cascade Books — © 2013 by Julie L. Moore.

Les Murray: All poems are included with permission of the poet. "Poetry and Religion" and "Easter 1984" are from *The Daylight Moon*. Copyright © 1987 by Les Murray. Reprinted with the permission of Persea Books, Inc (New York), www.perseabooks.com. The following poems—"Tired From Understanding" is from "Twelve Poems" from *The Biplane Houses* by Les Murray. Copyright © 2006 by Les Murray; «Poetry and Religion», «The Knockdown Question», «The Poisons of Right and Left», and «Church», are from *New Selected Poems*, by Les Murray; Copyright © 2007, 2012, 2014 by Les Murray; and "Jesus Was a Healer" is from *Waiting for the Past* by Les Murray; Copyright © 2015 by Les Murray - and are reprinted with permission of Carcanet Press Ltd., Farrar, Straus and Giroux, LLC and Margaret Connolly and Associates.

Marilyn Nelson: All poems are from *The Fields of Praise: New and Selected Poems* (1997) and are reprinted with permission from the poet and Louisiana State University Press.

Jae Newman: "Apartment Near Airport" first appeared in *Korean Quarterly*, "Unnamed" first appeared in *Tiger's Eye,* and "Canticle" first appeared in *Louisville Review*. All poems are reprinted with permission from the poet, and are from *Collage of Seoul* — Poiema Poetry Series/Cascade Books — © 2015 by Jae Newman.

Eric Pankey: All poems are reprinted with permission from the poet. "In Memory" and "In Sienna, Prospero Reconsiders the Marriage at Cana" from *The Pear as One Example: New and Selected Poems* 1984—2008. Copyright © 2008 by Eric Pankey. Reprinted with the permission of The Permissions Company, Inc., on behalf of Copper Canyon Press, www.coppercanyonpress.org.

Anne Porter: "Music" and "After Psalm 137" appeared in *Commonweal*. All poems are from *Living Things: Collected Poems* by Anne Porter. Reprinted with the permission from Steerforth Press.

Tania Runyan: All poems are reprinted with permission from the poet. "The Empty Tomb," which first appeared in *The Christian Century*, and "El Train Magnificat" by Tania Runyan, copyright © 2011 by Tania Runyan published in *A Thousand Vessels* (WordFarm, 2011). Used with permission from WordFarm. "Setting My Mind," "Put on the New Self" which first appeared in *The Christian Century*, "That Your Love May Abound" and "Before All Things" which first appeared in *Image* by Tania Runyan, copyright © 2013 by Tania Runyan published in *Second Sky* — Poiema Poetry Series/Cascade Books (2013).

Nicholas Samaras: All poems are reprinted with permission of the poet. Other than "Vespers" they are from *American Psalm, World Psalm* (Ashland Poetry Press, 2014) by Nicholas Samaras. "The Unpronounceable Psalm" first appeared in *Image*.

Martha Serpas: All poems are reprinted with permission of the poet. "As If There Were Only One" is from *Côte Blanche* by Martha Serpas (New Issues), "The Diener" and "Badlands" are from *The Diener* and are reprinted with permission of Louisisana State University Press (2015).

Luci Shaw: All poems are reprinted with permission from the poet. "Spring, St. Martin's Chapel, Cathedral of St. John the Divine" by Luci Shaw is from *Water Lines* (2003), and is reprinted with permission of William B. Eerdmans Publishing Company. "Present" by Luci Shaw, copyright © 2006 by Luci Shaw, published in *What the Light Was Like* (WordFarm, 2006); used with permission from WordFarm. "So It Is With the Spirit," "Mary Considers Her Situation," "Verb," "What I Needed To Do," "Collection, Recollection" and "Thunder and Then" by Luci Shaw, copyright © 2013 by Luci Shaw, published in *Scape*— Poiema Poetry Series/Cascade Books (2013).

Robert Siegel: "A Colt the Foal of an Ass" first appeared in *Stories for the Christian Year*. All poems are reprinted with permission from Ann Siegel, and are from *Within This Tree of Bones: New and Selected Poems* — Poiema Poetry Series/Cascade Books — © 2013 by Robert Siegel.

Anya Krugovoy Silver: "From Nothing" first appeared in *America*. All poems are reprinted with permission from the poet. The following poems are also reprinted with permission from Louisiana State University Press. "Persimmon" is from *The Ninety-Third Name of God* (2010). "Stage IV" and "No, It's Not" are from *I Watched You Disappear* (2014).

C.H. Sisson: All poems are from *Collected Poems*, copyright © 1998. Reprinted with permission of Carcanet Press Ltd.

Marjorie Stelmach: "Cellar Door" first appeared in *Image*, and is reprinted with the permission of the poet. It is from *Falter* — Poiema Poetry Series/Cascade Books — © 2016 by Marjorie Stelmach.

Margo Swiss: Both poems are reprinted with permission from the poet, and are from *The Hatching of the Heart* — Poiema Poetry Series/ Cascade Books — © 2015 by Margo Swiss.

Michael Symmons Roberts: All poems are reprinted with permission from the poet. "Jairus" and "Food for Risen Bodies II" are from *Corpus* by Michael Symmons Roberts, published by Jonathan Cape. Reproduced by permission of The Random House Group Ltd. "Compline" is from *Soft Keys* by Michael Symmons Roberts, published by Jonathan Cape. Reproduced by permission of The Random House Group Ltd.

Mary Szybist: "The Cathars Etc." and "Girls Overheard While Assembling a Puzzle," which first appeared in *The Kenyon Review*, are from *Incarnadine.* Copyright © 2012 by Mary Szybist. Reprinted with the permission of the poet, and The Permissions Company, Inc. on behalf of Graywolf Press, Minneapolis, Minnesota. www.graywolfpress.org

John Terpstra: "Near-Annunciation at Carroll's Point" and "New Year, Good Work" first appeared in *Image*. Reprinted with permission of the poet.

R.S. Thomas: All poems are from taken from *Collected Poems* 1945 — 1990 by R.S. Thomas, and are reprinted with permission from Orion Publishing Group.

Edwin Thumboo: Both poems are reprinted with permission from the poet, and are from *The Best of Edwin Thumboo* Epigram Books, © 2012, Edwin Thumboo.

Jeanne Murray Walker: All poems are reprinted with permission from the poet. "Bergman" and "Leaving The Planetarium" which both first appeared in *Image*, and "Staying Power" which first appeared in *Poetry*, are from *New Tracks, Night Falling* (2009). Reprinted with permission of William B. Eerdmans Publishing Co. "Miniature Psalm of Complaint," which first appeared in *Books and Culture,* by Jeanne Murray Walker. Copyright © 2014 by Jeanne Murray Walker. Published in *Helping the Morning: New and Selected Poems* (WordFarm, 2014). Used with permission from WordFarm. "In The Beginning Was The Word" also first appeared in *Image*.

Richard Wilbur: "Love Calls Us to the Things of this World," "A Wedding Toast," "Matthew VIII, 28 ff" and "A Christmas Hymn" are from *COLLECTED POEMS:* 1943—2004 by Richard Wilbur. Copyright ©

2004 by Richard Wilbur. Reprinted by permission of Houghton Mifflin Harcourt Publishing Company. All rights reserved.

Paul J. Willis: All poems are reprinted with permission from the poet. "Rosing From The Dead" which first appeared in *Christianity and Literature* and "The Good Portion" by Paul J. Willis, copyright © 2009 by Paul J, Willis. Used with permission from WordFarm. are from *Rosing From The Dead* (2009). Used with permission from WordFarm. "Christmas Child" which first appeared in *Lamp-Post*, "Intercession" and "Listen," which both first appeared in *The Christian Century,* by Paul J. Willis , copyright © 2014 by Paul J, Willis. are from *Say This Prayer Into The Past* — Poiema Poetry Series/Cascade Books (2014).

Rowan Williams: All poems are reprinted with permission from the poet, and are from *The Poems of Rowan Williams*, copyright © 2014. Reprinted with permission of Carcanet Press Ltd.

Christian Wiman: Thanks to the poet for assistance and permission for including the following poems. "Every Riven Thing," "This Mind of Dying," and "When the Time's Toxins" from EVERY RIVEN THING by Christian Wiman. Copyright © 2011 by Christian Wiman. Reprinted by permission of Farrar, Straus and Giroux, LLC.

"Coming Into the Kingdom" and "Witness" from ONCE IN THE WEST by Christian Wiman. Copyright © 2014 by Christian Wiman. Reprinted by permission of Farrar, Straus and Giroux, LLC.

COLLECTIONS IN THIS SERIES INCLUDE:

Made in the USA
Middletown, DE
09 May 2018